DISAPPEARING
PERSONS

SUNY series in Psychoanalysis and Culture
Henry Sussman, editor

DISAPPEARING PERSONS

Shame and Appearance

Benjamin Kilborne

STATE UNIVERSITY OF NEW YORK PRESS

Published by
State University of New York Press, Albany

For information, address State University of New York Press,
90 State Street, Suite 700, Albany, NY 12207

Production by Christine L. Hamel
Marketing by Fran Keneston

Library of Congress Cataloging-in-Publication Data

Kilborne, Benjamin.
    Disappearing persons : shame and appearance / by Benjamin Kilborne.
        p. cm.
    Includes bibliographical references (p.) and index.
    ISBN 0-7914-5199-2 (alk. paper) — ISBN 0-7914-5200-X (pbk. : alk. paper)
        1. Psychoanalysis. 2. Shame. 3. Conflict (Psychology) 4. Body image. I. Title.

BF173 .K432 2002
152.4—dc21
                                                                    2001020754

10 9 8 7 6 5 4 3 2 1

Contents

    Deceit and Remedies by Still More Deceit   37

    Shame and Aidos   38
    Shame and the Sneeze: the Analysis of Mark   39
    Deception, Outrage, and Remedy by Even
        More Deceit   41
    The Vain Invention of the Onlooker   43

4. What Do You See Me to Be?
    Invisibility and Performance   45

    Exposure and Invisibility: Adam   46
    Spy Glass Hill and the "Rage of Personality:"
        Adam, Graham Greene, and Kim Philby   48
    Oedipal Shame, Spies and Fantasy   51
    Recognizing Choice in the Unseen   52
    Of Oedipal Blindness and Oedipal Shame:
        Loss, Disappearance, and Rage   53
    The Hunger Artist   55
    Shame and Performance Anxiety:
        A Shamed Violinist Plays to a Lion   56
    Shame and Creativity   59

5. I Can't See; I'm Invisible   61

    When I Don't See You I Can Invent You Better:
        The Analysis of Susan   63
    Do You Want Me To Be Someone Else?   65
    Peek-a-boo, Disappearance, and the Game
        of the Bobbin   66
    I Am Invisible; I Can't See Myself   68
    Seeing, Being Seen, and Matters of Privacy   69

6. What the Camera Sees:
    The Tragedy of Modern Heroes and
    "The Rules of the Game"   73

    Free Association and Open Form   75
    Of Disguises, Mechanisms, and Music Boxes   77
    Everyone Has His Reasons   78
    Deceit, Denial, Honor, and the Rules of the Game   80

Acknowledgments

This book has been so long in gestation and the difficulties in being born have been so bewildering and painful, that it would never have survived but for a number of generous spirited friends to whom I owe its appearance: Donald Lamm saw in the early stages of the project something worth encouraging; Melvin Lansky and Andrew Morrison provided friendship, writings, warmth, dedication to analytic work, and companionship in running the "Shame Dynamics" workshop at the biannual meetings of the American Psychoanalytic Association; Leon Wurmser's stature and work in shame have served as beacons, his friendship and vision have been so valuable; Bennett Simon's erudition and analytic heart and spirit proved to be such a source of hope in dark times; Robert Benson, Werner Muensterberger, and Douglas Schave stood by the project even when it was incomprehensible; Joseph Adamson's work on Melville and shame reminded me that what I was doing might be of interest to those in literary studies. His support, continued interest, and enthusiasm over the years has meant so much. Ursula Mahlendorf suggested fewer literary examples and more interpretative context; Marion Fabe's experience in film encouraged my writing of the chapter on "The Rules of the Game"; Melford Spiro's friendship and encouragement were so heartening; Stephen Rosenblum enjoined me to be more clinical; Paul Schwaber suggested that with respect to Pirandello I be more ready to "murder my darlings"; Anna-Maria Rizzuto encouraged me to pursue a phenomenological approach to analytic work; William Kilborne Jr.'s brotherly functions extended to a particular keenness of editorial eye and a willingness to read not one but many drafts; Allerton Kilborne knows so well what this book is about and has provided affectionate encouragement right from the start; Eve Wood,

ix

whose prodigious gifts as a poet helped nudge me toward greater clarity of expression (and whose poems gave me a chance to see how feelings underlying the book could be imagined); Philip Blumberg provided breadth of vision and encouragement at a crucial time; Michael Gilsenan, without whose friendship I don't know what I would have done, spent hours at the Happy Pancake, his head full of opera, pouring over early drafts. I also would like to thank the three anonymous readers for State University of New York Press who contributed fine and thoughtful reviews; James Peltz, an editor of gracious manner and watchful eye; Christine Hamel, who kept the book on track; Jane Kerner whose friendship and editorial labors saved me from shame; and, most of all, my patients.

Preface

This book has been more than a decade in the making and has gone through countless transformations out of which, I hope, the contours of a landscape can now appear. Trained in literature, history, anthropology, and clinical psychoanalysis, I have drawn upon our humanistic tradition to describe a psychocultural crisis. My basic thesis is neither original nor startling: that we attempt to control the way we feel by controlling the way we appear. However, the effort to link this thesis to notions of shame and conflict represents, I think, a new direction of inquiry.[1]

Let me say a word about my methods. First, the book was born from clinical difficulties: how to identify, describe, and work through psychological processes responsible for repression and self-censorship that I came to associate with shame dynamics, idealization, and Oedipal conflict. My patients who drew me to these struggles have continually heartened and moved me by their perseverance and courage in pursuing their analyses even through excruciating confusion, anguish, and despair (the sickness unto death of which Kierkegaard speaks). Pieces of their analyses appear throughout this book. Although my theoretical orientation as a clinician is phenomenological, drive-oriented, and conflictual, I have avoided theoretical debates and recondite terminology in an effort to tell a story and to place my investigations in a broader context. While I hope the description of psychodynamics retains all the necessary twists and turns to be valuable to psychoanalysts and psychotherapists, I also hope the book can be accessible to university students and to a wide range of readers.

In the sense in which Sigmund Freud used the term, my method of investigation was *psychoanalytic*: without psychoanalytic methods and a clinical setting I could not have defined my field. Psycho-analytic practice was therefore indispensable to me in coming to know my subject. But the exploration of these dynamics could not, I thought, be restricted to the scope of psychoanalysis alone. As an anthropologist I had some understanding of how important cultural processes are to the adequate grasp of individual psychodynamics, and vice versa. I was fortunate in being able to draw on the writings of teachers and friends like Margaret Mead, George Devereux, Weston LaBarre, and Melford Spiro. Using the work of anthropolo-gists, social theorists, and philosophers, as well as my clinical back-ground, I was able to shuttle back and forth between individual and social phenomena which, as Devereux emphasized, are essentially complementary rather than antithetical. Also, narratives are the stuff of my book, so that it may better speak and express, rather than merely designate, what it is about.

As I began what was to be this book I found myself irresistibly drawn to the work of Luigi Pirandello because of the way in which he treats the subject of appearance and our reliance on it. Readers of early drafts of this manuscript wondered whether it was not a book about Pirandello. I did not think it was supposed to be. I was striv-ing to understand psychodynamics and tragic conflicts organized around appearances to which my clinical work had drawn my atten-tion. Pirandello's work helped me explore and try out my ideas about shame, conflict, and appearance. Not only that, but I could feel in his work, and in other works of literature, the urgency and pain of what I was trying to describe. In a sense, Pirandello kept me from letting theory, like the yellow pages, do the walking.

Finally, two decades living in Los Angeles, after raising a child in Paris, provided me with contrasts that I have yet fully to understand. While Paris never ceases to amaze me with its beauty and the density of human experiences and associations, Los Angeles lives on illusions and chimera, and offers reassurance that nothing is ever as it appears.

What emerged, therefore, was a book using literature to think about psychodynamic concepts, and psychoanalytic questions in reading literature. If from one vantage point, the pages that follow are a hybrid of applied literature and applied psychoanalysis, from another they are an attempt on the part of a clinician to bring appearance anxiety and Oedipal shame alive by relating them to our humanistic tradition and vice versa. The result, I hope, you will find engaging, moving, and thought-provoking.

Introduction

Self esteem is the secure feeling that no one, as yet, is suspicious.

—H. L. Mencken

At the climax of *Oedipus Rex*, the play of Sophocles that Aristotle uses as the prototype of tragedy in his *Poetics*, Oedipus, confronted with the suicide by hanging of his wife and mother Jocasta, takes the golden broaches on her robe and plunges their spikes deep into his eyes, wailing,

No longer, my eyes, shall you behold the horror
I suffered and performed. Too long
have you looked on those on whom you should not have looked
while failing to see what you should have seen.
Henceforth therefore, be dark.

It is this apogee of the tragic situation that we take as our starting point. Oedipus cannot stand to look at what he has done; if he does, he must suffer the agonizing and intolerable pain of having been so blind to his own fate and to himself, and having wrought destruction upon Thebes at the very time he believed he was establishing order and dominion. Having realized how blindly he has lived, in rage, humiliation, and despair he forces blindness upon himself. The tragedy of Oedipus stems not only from the horror and guilt over acts unwittingly committed (killing his father and marrying his mother); it stems also—and perhaps more fundamentally still—from

1

his own blindness to who he is: a man who in infancy was abandoned by his parents, his feet pierced, and his death entrusted to a shepherd who, unable to execute his task, left him helpless in the wild.

Like Ajax, who at the opening of the Sophocles play by that name[2] is tricked by Apollo into believing that a flock of sheep are his enemies, and who when he realizes that he has been duped, cannot bear his shame, Oedipus suffers mortifying defeat. Not only has he been blind, but, worse, his blindness has made a mockery of his aspirations and appearance by showing them publicly to be vain. When Oedipus can no longer "not know" what he has done, when he becomes aware of his role in the Theban plague that as king he has publicly declared he will alleviate, he blinds himself. It is not enough that he be either ostracized or that he banish himself (i.e., that he be isolated), since the more essential conflict—and human dilemma— has to do with his relation to himself. By conflating as it does psychic and physical blindness, the self-inflicted punishment of Oedipus expresses a feeling that he cannot bear imagining himself in the eyes of others, and therefore must blot them out by "really" making himself blind. When he says "Henceforth be dark," he is expressing suicidal, annihilatory rage at others who "see through" him, and is attacking what links him to society and to other human beings.[3]

Oedipal defeat (unfair competition and humiliating impotence) cannot easily be separated from Oedipal rage, as the Sophocles play illustrates so well. Even though Oedipus is king, he still must contend with his abandonment as a child, with the shame of his Oedipal victory (killing his father and sleeping with his mother), and with the resounding defeat implicit in his inability to slay the monster of the plague and so demonstrate to the people of Thebes that he is a capable defender. His shameful defeat and humiliation as a king echoes the grief and humiliation he suffered as an infant. It is this grief, humiliation, and pain—the pain of having had cruel, abandoning parents who left him to die—which makes his Oedipal shame impossibly toxic, and that summons the depths of his rage.

Freud interpreted *Oedipus Rex* to be concerned with guilt, and guilt with aggression.[4] Analysts since have tended to associate the Oedipus complex with drives (i.e., the wish to sleep with Mother and murder Father along with the defenses that such impulses engender). Then in the 1970s Heinz Kohut and the Self-Psychologists emphasized deficit rather than guilt, the failure of ego-ideals rather than aggression, pre-Oedipal as opposed to Oedipal dynamics. But there is no need to look at psychodynamics as Manichean, as *either* one *or* the other, since to do so needlessly limits the scope of analytic work.[5]

In terms of sociocultural analyses, Ruth Benedict (1946), E. R. Dodds (1951), J. B. Peristiany (1965), G. Piers and M. Singer (1953), and others have pursued an either/or approach to the subject, distinguishing between guilt-based cultures and shame-based ones. This too is an unnecessary dichotomy. We will see that guilt and shame exist side by side, as do aggression and deficit, in a range of combinations. No culture is exclusively one or the other. In many recent works, for example Richard Wollheim's *On The Emotions,* guilt and shame as "so-called moral emotions" are treated together and not distinguished at all.

Bearing in mind the shame/guilt continuum, and how much one can hide the other, I will focus on the spectrum of shame phenomena, particularly on Oedipal shame: on feelings of profound defeat (failed competition), annihilatory self-criticism (failed self-worth), helplessness (failed cries for help), rage, and basic threats to self-image and psychic viability. I will be concerned with establishing the relationship between Oedipal shame and appearance anxiety, oscillating in my analysis from individual psychodynamics to cultural phenomena.

OEDIPAL SHAME AND THE ORIGINS OF APPEARANCE ANXIETY

Oedipus puts out his eyes because he cannot tolerate seeing others looking at him in scorn and derision; he cannot bear having failed in so monumental a fashion, and wishes never again to see himself. The appearance he has wished to convey has failed miserably; he is shown up to be altogether other than what he pretended to be. Instead of feeling victorious over his father (who he did not know was his father) and triumphant that he has possessed his mother (who he did not know was his mother), he is held up to the eyes of the multitude as a pawn of fate. Is there not far more to Oedipal conflict than an internalized conflict between parents, one of whom is a sexual object and the other a rival?

Why does Oedipus attack his own eyes? In the studies of infant development, the infant looks into his mother's eyes, depending upon her responses in order to feel at ease in the world. If the mother does not respond, the infant bursts into tears. T. B. Brazelton (see Tronick, Wise, and Brazelton, 1978) and others (e.g., V. Demos, 1993) have demonstrated that a lack of response on the part of the mother produces first anger, then depression as the infant gives up and turns against the wall.

What is the mother responding (or not responding) to? Mothers are not likely to ever provide satisfactory answers. Clearly the infants can never tell us. As soon as the infant can look in the direction of his mother, she fantasizes what he sees, who he is, and who he will become. The infant responds to his mother's fantasies of how she appears to him, fantasies that ineluctably become a part of infant's world, and with respect to which he must get his bearings. Correspondingly the infant struggles to know what his mother is experiencing, and the infant's struggles are picked up consciously and unconsciously by his mother. In this way, the infant's responses contribute to the shaping of the mother's fantasies about him and about herself as a mother.[6] By the time the infant is four or five months old, the mother already has a history of her fantasies about how she is being looked at by her child, and already has a history of her attempts to control how she is being seen so as to control her own feelings toward her child and toward herself. And by this time the infant has a stake in helping his mother feel as she wants to feel in relation to him. This is the infant's way of trying to make the world a safe place.

In short, on the basis of innate strivings the infant "invents" his mother at the same time as he "invents" himself and the world. Out of the bits and pieces of his interactions with her, using what he can understand (this includes what he can imagine) of his mother's values and fears as she relates to him, the child cobbles together a sense of himself and the world. And where his mother fails to provide the child with the necessary comfort and security, the child fantasizes the circumstances under which she might give him what he needs. The infant's sense of self thus includes both perceptions and fantasies of himself and his world, and of his mother. The inventions and fantasies of parent and child lay the groundwork for feelings and ideals of beauty, order, and well-being. Psychoanalysts have long spoken of the relation between idealization and shame. Shame can motivate children to idealize their parents, and shame can result if they cannot do so (i.e., by making parents better than they are).

When Oedipus blinds himself, he disappears from his own sight by making the world dark. Like Oedipus, those who cannot tolerate the shame of their injuries and grief doom themselves to cycles of shame, imposture, and rage. The angrier they become about their shame, the more flagrant will discrepancies between views and versions of who they are appear to them.[7] And the more obsessed they will become with fantasies of appearance and anxiety over disappearing.

APPEARANCE ANXIETY AS A CULTURAL PHENOMENON

At the end of the millennium, there is increasing anxiety about appearances, and there are, inevitably, cultural responses to such anxieties. Anxiety over appearance has often been related to photography and the media, to the world of fashion, public relations and image making, plastic surgery, bodybuilding, cosmetics, television, and all those means on which we rely to appear as we wish, to give ourselves the feeling that we control the way others see us. By controlling how we appear to others, we try to control how we appear (and feel) to ourselves. In one sense the dichotomies between public and private spheres of our lives may be said to depend upon culturally shared illusions of mastery, and these, in turn, upon appearances. Paradoxically, the very effectiveness of technology and medicine, the very power produced by painkilling drugs and anesthesia, contributes to illusions of power and permanence that hold at bay fears of pain, helplessness, need, vulnerability, and shame required for responsive, responsible human interactions.

APPEARANCE ANXIETY, OBSERVATION, AND PERCEPTION

The social sciences distinguishes sharply between observer and observed; the dialectics of "observation" entail looking.[8] Yet disciplines relying upon participant observation often neglect the fact that those observed look back, and that the dynamics of scrutiny work both ways.[9] Studies of cannibalism put a crimp in assumptions about the virtues of participant observation.

Some social theorists have suggested that shame is the social glue holding society together. In his classic study on the gift, which is implicitly a study in competition and appearance, Marcel Mauss, Emile Durkheim's nephew, speaks of shame and the loss of face for the Chinese, the Kwakiutl, and Haida, American Indian of the northwest coast, for whom "to lose face is to lose one's spirit, which is truly the 'face,' the dancing mask, the right to incarnate a spirit and wear an emblem or totem."[10] For some people and patients (e.g., Susan in chapter 5), it means losing the shape of an intelligible world and of one's own being, and therefore feeling annihilatory disorganization and isolation. For Mauss, what maintains "face" is, implicitly, the social bond, represented as a prestation, a mutual obligation, without which the individual disappears.

Analysts try to understand how patients rely upon appearances and what this means. Naturally this includes both how they appear to their patients and how they wish to appear themselves. Unanalyzed shame in the analyst makes it difficult or impossible to interpret defensive shame spirals in the patient. Shame misunderstood or avoided contributes to destructiveness and grief in all human relations.

SEEING, KNOWING, IMAGE, AND APPEARANCE

Reliance upon appearances entails hiding whatever appearances one finds unacceptable, a reaction we associate with shame. Interestingly, the word *shame* is derived from the Indo-European root *skam* or *skem*, meaning "to hide." From this same root come our two words *skin* and *hide*. Just as the notion of "grace" designates a feeling that God approves of what he sees, the concept of "dis-grace" designates a feeling of disapproval, an experience that others—who have seen how we have disgraced ourselves—are looking on with contempt and scorn.

Since Plato, "seeing" has been used as a metaphor for understanding ("reflective" thinking), and has been strongly reinforced by cultural ideas of the imagination (derived from the same root as "image"), and by metaphors such as "the light of reason" or the "Enlightenment."[11] In making the distinction between the visible and the invisible,[12] Plato and those who followed him have been speaking not about what the eye actually sees, but rather about the imagination, or that faculty that allows us to "see." Plato's mind's eye sees only when it can imagine the ideals or essences in terms of which to make sense of perceptions, a point conveyed by the allegory of the cave in the *Republic*. For Plato, thinking and seeing are comparable processes; light and truth, therefore functionally equivalent.[13] Along these same lines, Leonardo da Vinci believed that understanding comes to us through seeing and imagining. Leonardo's emphasis on the profound links between seeing, knowing, and the imagination, also a hallmark of Renaissance humanism, has not only influenced our artistic tradition,[14] but simultaneously contributed to the rise of empiricism and to basic assumptions about scientific investigation and the nature of evidence.[15]

We can recognize the presence of appearance anxiety in debates over both the nature of perception and definitions of the mind/body problem. After Galileo, rationality and vision became peculiarly allied against bodily feelings (e.g., Descartes, Spinoza, and Kant). It became easier to put aside reverence for the human body as God's creation, and to focus more exclusively on yearnings for something pure and untainted by bodily confusion and mortality. After World War I Gestaltists reframed the mind/body problem by focusing on perception and the psychological process of closure.[16] For any perception to be "significative" there must be a "ground" against which it can be perceived, and in that endeavor lie basic epistemological difficulties about which Jean-Paul Sartre and Maurice Merleau-Ponty disagreed all their lives. In *Le visible et l'invisible*, Merleau-Ponty describes a phenomenology of the imaginary, of the hidden, of the invisible that would then be perceived as part of the phenomenology of what can be seen.[17]

Not surprisingly our Judeo-Christian tradition, which has always emphasized the eyes of the soul, has had similar difficulties with the problematic nature of seeing and being seen (e.g., the divine power of God's "all-seeing" eye, and the prohibition against looking that can be represented by the eye on our dollar bill). In ancient Judaism not only could one not look at the covenant, one was not supposed to know there was nothing in it. Taboos against graven images thus may be related to the wish to look and the vulnerability (the shame) of being humiliated in the eyes of God, whoever God is imagined to be.

OEDIPUS, SHAME, AND THE VOID OF AVOIDANCE

As long as Oedipus can avoid his fate by seeing himself in the eyes of the admiring people of Thebes, as long as he can rely on others not to see what he cannot admit, he can continue to function.[18] Far from being the king and savior of the Theban people, Oedipus is their scourge because of what he does not, and will not, see. Oedipus snuffs out the world by attacking his eyes; dishonored by being abandoned by his own parents, he becomes dishonorable by blindly attempting to defy fate. Within our Western tradition, ignorance, "not-seeing" is often felt to be a shameful indication of some basic flaw (e.g., Adam and Eve or Oedipus), and can be reinforced and further complicated by reliance upon someone else not to see what one does not want to acknowledge. Seen in this light, the emphasis on appearance in our culture serves to nourish the illusion that we can *really* control what others see and do not see of us. How much more comfortable to avoid having others see how little we know ourselves, to prevent others from seeing bits of us of which we are not aware, to disown and avoid what we do not see in ourselves, what others would not want to have us be, and what we cannot tolerate being.

The plight of Oedipus is ours. When we cannot bear our shame we too try to avoid or evacuate what we are ashamed of, and to ward off the humiliation of having been defeated in a conflict we could not understand. And when the confrontation with blindness to what others see and to what we know becomes unbearable, the result is horror, dread, rage, despair, and isolation, as it is for Oedipus. By disavowing what is shameful, our contemporary emphasis on appearance creates a void, which must be concealed all the more desperately, thereby doing profound violence to our confidence in who we are, and to our ability to see and to bear the pain and suffering inherent in the human condition.

1 The Contempt of the Queen's Dwarf

On Psychic Size

Nothing angered and mortified me so much as the Queen's dwarf, who being of the lowest stature that was ever in that country (for I verily think he was not full thirty foot high) became so insolent at seeing a creature so much beneath him that he would always affect to swagger and look big as he passed by me . . . and he seldom failed of a smart word or two upon my littleness.

—Jonathan Swift, *Gulliver's Travels*

PSYCHIC SIZE AND SELF-REGARD

In Lewis Carroll's *Alice in Wonderland*, Alice falls down the well, reaches the bottom, and attempts to change her size by drinking the contents of a bottle marked "Drink Me." She feels herself shrinking.[1] "What a curious feeling," she exclaims. "I must be shutting up like a telescope." In the light of the dialectics of looking (i.e., imagining others seeing and not seeing), the image of a telescope makes *very* good sense. And in case the reader does not get the point, Carroll has Alice then decide to eat a cake in order to assume her "normal" size. "Curiouser and curiouser!" cried Alice, "Now I'm opening out like the largest telescope that ever was. Good-bye feet." Thereafter there is no way Alice can "fit in," being always either too large or too small.

Alice is doomed to being conspicuous and, to those around her, "not-us." In the same way, the Wonderland creatures are, for her, doomed to being "not-me." She cannot recognize herself in them and they cannot recognize themselves in her. This unrecognizability, this anxiety over never being able to imagine oneself through the eyes of others, drives the entire book. With the aid of absurdity Carroll warms us up to his uneasy magic, and makes identity confusion more palatable. As Alice struggles to "find" herself in those around her, her very attempts become absurd. When the Caterpillar asks insistently, "Who are you?" the question appears outlandish, nightmarish, and impossible to answer.

There is no way Alice can really get her bearings from the world around her, no way she can imagine how she might better control her appearance. Therefore she retreats into assumptions about the way one behaves, an etiquette distinctly out of place. Rather than feeling anxious, Alice seems to be smugly convinced that Wonderland is nothing other than it appears to be: nonsensical.

As a fundamental experience and notion through which we perceive relationships, psychic size is an internal or shared experience of *relative* size, dependent upon standards of judgment and comparison. Consider, for example, our word *self-regard* in the light of the French word *le regard*, "the look." "Self-regard," wrote Freud, "appears to us to be an expression of the size of the ego."[2] Here, I think, Freud is speaking not of objective size, but rather of proportion. For him the ego must be big enough to be able to hold its own against the (sometimes combined) forces of the id and superego. Speaking of the dynamic nature of proportion and of what feels right, Rudolf Arnheim suggests that "rightness presents itself not as dead immobility but as the active equipoise of concerted forces, while wrongness is seen as a struggle to get away from an unsatisfactory state."[3]

ASCLEPIUS, THE TALL MAN, AND LITTLE PEOPLE

Representations of size have always been important. In ancient Egypt royal figures were always far larger than anyone else. And in ancient Greece and in the Mediterranean basin generally, dreamers were visited by the "tall man," the hallmark of royal messenger dreams. At the opening of the dream, the "tall man" stood at the head of the dreamer, who was below him lying down. Only after the tall man identified the dreamer, saying, "So-and-So you are asleep," could the dream proper begin. Such narrative conventions served to set the dream apart from ordinary experience, to conventionalize communication between gods and humans, and to underscore the status of humans when compared to gods and their messengers. Towering dream figures in Greek literature indicate relative status, reminding mortals once again by their presence how great are the gods.

These narrative conventions can be found also among worshipers of the cult of Asclepius, the most prevalent religion in the early Christian period and the one considered to present the greatest threat to burgeoning Christianity. Asclepius, the god of healing associated with the caduceus, symbol of the medical profession, appeared in curative dreams precisely as did the "tall man" in ancient Greece.[4] Ailing pilgrims would dream that the god of healing towered over them. He would then proceed to take out his knife and to operate on them, to give them advice, or in some way to ease their afflictions. Might the psychoanalytic positions (analyst sitting in chair able to see patient, patient lying on couch unable to see analyst) have been influenced by the Asclepian tradition? Freud was familiar with it and might well have identified himself with Asclepius. Perhaps too this tradition of curative dreams contributed to the development of Freud's concept of the transference, a major feature of which is dreaming of the analyst.

Throughout the world, beliefs in the truth of dreams and in the scale of dreamed gods lend further weight to the psychological importance of scale and psychic size. For instance, in his *Pygmies and Dream Giants* Kilton Stewart describes in great detail the dreams of a Philippino group of pygmies, who dream of giants as large as he.

Common figures of speech provide us with ample evidence that much of our evaluation of ourselves depends upon comparing ourselves with others. Consider, for example, expressions such as "a tall order," "small-minded," or the very clear relation conveyed by the expression "to look down on someone" or "to look down one's nose at someone." The list goes on to include "that was big (or small) of him," "high office," "high-minded," "low brow," and "lower (or upper) class." In the Greek tradition Olympian beings tower over the lot of us mortals, as we were towered over by our parents when we were small. We "look up to" these Olympian beings, whether parental or mythical. Consider the very ideas of "smallness" and of "largeness" as qualities derived from our experiences as infants and children in the process of "growing up." Note, we do not "grow down." "Upness" is associated with growth, and things everyone aspires to. We want to "live up"[5] to the expectations both of ourselves and of others.

While the ancient Greeks prized such differences and comparisons in size, the Christian world, by contrast, avoided them. Not only did the injunction against graven images make God impossible to "size up," since there is no way of measuring up to what one cannot see, but it was held that any comparison of man's physical size to God was reprehensible. So great was God that intimations of comparison could be dismissed as blasphemy. Renaissance humanism grappled with the central place previously given to God, and made Man the center of the constructed universe, symbolized by Leonardo Da Vinci's figure inscribed in geometric forms. Man became, at least in principle, the measure of the universe.

While we experience our size in relation to important persons in our lives, this experience is rooted in bodily sensation.[6] Psychic size strikes root in bodily memories, in childhood experiences, and in family relationships. It affects not only the perception and experience of one's physical body, but also the perception and experience of one's family. Conversely, family dynamics of idealization, competition, hostility, envy, and shame affect the experience of psychic size. As our bodies change, as we grow, our size changes; as we grow we "size" ourselves, trying on images of ourselves "for size." One very tall (6'3") patient in his early twenties commented about a girlfriend, "I've known her since I was five feet tall."

Sometimes the physical size of our mythical beings (e.g., Gargantua and Paul Bunyan) can be a defense against feeling "belittled." Or diminutive persons can serve as symbols for those who feel belittled, as is the case of The Little People in Ireland, and of various other fictitious beings who are imagined to be *significantly* (as opposed to insignificantly) small. Thus the positive or negative value placed upon being large or small is distinct from actual size. "Oversize" persons often feel no less anxious about their size than those who are unusually small. To these "sizings" must be added persons with body image distortions (e.g., those with eating disorders). Being large can be perceived both as an asset and a basic flaw. Similarly, being small can be a symbol of endearment (my little chickadee and *mon petit chou*) and a symbol of insignificance. Once again here, the primary reality is psychic reality.[7]

Paul Schilder and other psychoanalysts have emphasized that, like all perception,[8] seeing depends upon bodily (e.g., haptic) feelings, memories, images, experiences, and values. Schilder uses the term *body image* to designate "the picture of our own body that we form in our mind, that is to say, the way in which the body appears to ourselves."[9] This self-appearance is constructed through experiences both internal (e.g., pain and illness, and satisfaction and pleasure) and in relation to others. Furthermore, as a construction,[10] self-appearance is never stable. It is always changing. As such it is a potential source of anxiety.

BROBDINGNAG AND LILLIPUT

In *Gulliver's Travels* Jonathan Swift freely plays with the dynamics of size, describing *feelings* of largeness and smallness, helplessness, competition, envy, rage, and shame. Like Carroll after him, Swift makes use of comparison to underscore the human reliance on others. Ingeniously Swift describes Gulliver's reactions to scale depending upon the size of the inhabitants whose country he is visiting, either one-twelfth the size of ordinary mortals (in Lilliput) or twelve times their size (in Brobdingnag). No matter what Gulliver's size, Swift scales Gulliver's perceptions of the lands and seas he visits as faithfully as a mapmaker. Remember, for example, the scene in which Gulliver finds himself in Brobdingnag, in a field of reapers, about to be stepped on. The towering figure closest was "as tall as an ordinary spire-steeple," "took about ten yards at every stride," and spoke "in a voice many degrees louder than a speaking trumpet."[11] When this reaper came close, Gulliver felt utterly diminutive, powerless, terrified of being crushed by a being so gigantic he (the giant) would not even know he had eliminated a life from the face of the earth. The situation can be compared to a very small bug about to be sat on by a heavyweight champion.

In the words of Gulliver,

> I lamented my own folly and willfulness in attempting a second voyage against the advice of all my friends and relations. In this terrible agitation of mind I could not forbear thinking of Lilliput, whose inhabitants looked upon me as the greatest prodigy

that ever appeared in the world. . . . I reflected what a mortification it must prove to me to appear as inconsiderable in this
nation as one single Lilliputian would appear among us.[12]

In his terror, Gulliver does what we often do when experiencing
ourselves as diminutive: we imagine a time when we could "lord it over"
others, be they baby sisters, brothers, animals, or teddy bears—in short,
whoever can be relied upon to make us feel larger by comparison. And
Swift adds, "Undoubtedly philosophers are in the right when they tell us
that nothing is great or little otherwise than by comparison."[13] In other
words, what we "see" is always driven by what we "imagine"; imagination feeds on comparison, and comparison affects perception.

Whereas in Lilliput Gulliver (The Gigantic) is sought after by the
navy, able to determine the outcome of battles, and prized for his
strength and size, in Brobdingnag Gulliver (The Diminutive) is a toy of
the Queen and of children: to be played with but not taken seriously.
In Lilliput, he is envied; in Brobdingnag, he is constantly humiliated
and made to feel utterly insignificant. The envious Lilliputians try to
put Gulliver's eyes out while he is drugged, on the principle that if he
does not see them, he cannot perceive them to be small. If he does not
see how small they are, then they can be as large as they wish, avoiding the humiliation of seeing themselves through his eyes. Similarly,
some parents cannot stand children who might humiliate them by
being unlike them; a dwarf couple in Irvine, California, wanted to
abort a child who would have been normal height, and in Ohio a deaf
couple did not want a child who could hear.[14] Swift's own unhappy
childhood without a father and his discomfort with his own birthday
(he always fasted, mourned, and read the Book of Job) suggest motives
for self-magnification: "his dread lest he should fail in rivalry and in
strife with other men and his impotence with women."[15] The Oedipal
shame with which Swift and Carroll struggled in reality can be felt in
metaphors of size instability in both *Gulliver's Travels* and *Alice*.[16]

LARGE OR SMALL WE ARE ONLY BY COMPARISON

Smallness in fantasy can be not only a throwback to childhood experiences of being small and constantly "overlooked," but also a
defense against feeling large, powerful, and threatening. Just as one
can feel large so as not to feel insignificant and powerless, one can

feel small so as not to feel dangerous.[17] Thus, fantasies of either smallness or largeness can express both helplessness and rage.

In my work with patients I have found it common for my patients to attribute unexpected meanings to my size. While I may be used to my height (6'3") and take it for granted, Susan, an analytic patient who was diminutive in stature (barely 5'), constantly put the discrepancy in size to use. She resented having to "look up" to me, wanting herself to be autonomous and independent. For her my being tall was an affront to her desire to be "grown up."[18] When I went away for a few days, she dreamed:

> I was pregnant. I had not gained much weight, and the affair was painless. The baby was born and weighed something like three pounds. But when it was born it began shrinking until it was no larger than a dip stick. I wrapped it up in paper, but kept forgetting it and feared it would get sat on. It looked like a cartoon character.

After my absence, Susan dreams of having a baby that shrinks rather alarmingly, and is in danger of being forgotten or sat on. Her fear of dwindling carries with it anxiety over recognizing the size of her need for me, and anxiety too over not being able to maintain her size in my absence, of feeling literally diminished.[19] In this case, then, *physical* differences in size gave scope for *fantasized* feelings (e.g., of insignificance) which occupied an important place in the transference. She expected me to help her fend these feelings off, since she associated being male with being powerful, and being female with being helpless. She wanted to be able to depend upon my power without herself feeling helpless. In short, Susan's *physical* experience of her size in relation to me bore the hallmarks of fantasies about her own womanhood and my manhood, together with what these meant to her in terms of protection and autonomy, dominance and submission, power and helplessness, and vulnerability and rage.[20]

LITERARY LITTLENESS AND MINIATURIZATION

A discussion of size symbolism would be incomplete without a short consideration of the subject of smallness in English literature. Swift, of course, always had a fascination with littleness, expressed pithily in these immortal lines.[21]

So, Nat'ralists observe, a Flea
Hath smaller Fleas that on him prey,
And these have smaller Fleas to bite 'em
And so proceed ad infinitum

Charles Dickens[22] speaks of Mrs. Chirrup as "a pocket edition of the young man's best companion—a little woman at very high pressure, with an amazing quantity of goodness and usefulness in an exceedingly small space."[23] In *Our Mutual Friend*, Mrs. Peecher is "a little pincushion, a little housewife, a little book, a little workbox, a little set of tables and weights and measures, and a little woman, all in one."[24] Implied here is a link between smallness and accessibility, such that a small woman (Little Dorrit) can somehow be more complete than one existing on a grander scale. One thinks also of the tiny scale of the Bronte manuscripts (so small as to require a magnifying glass), in keeping with the scale of their toy soldiers. It has been suggested[25] that for the Bronte sisters smallness was a compromise formation, allowing them the grandeur of authorship while at the same time avoiding the critical eye of their father. What he could not read, he could not look down upon.

AMPLIFICATIO AND DEFENSES AGAINST DIMINISHMENT

Thomas Hobbes and other writers of the seventeenth century spoke of *Amplificato*, the technique of augmenting or diminishing crucial issues. *Amplificato* can serve as a useful concept in thinking about the dynamics of shame-driven distortions in the transference. Patients (and sometimes analysts) wish to be seen in what is assumed to be the most favorable light; each patient relies upon the analyst to assist in maintaining the wished-for version of the self (or, conversely, in hiding those portions of the self one does not want anyone to see). Inevitable difficulties arise, however, if to accomplish this, the patient enlists the analyst in defending against unwanted feelings.

For example, a patient of mine in his late twenties who came to me because of anxiety, crippling sexual inhibitions, an inability to complete projects, and a writing inhibition, repeatedly canceled sessions at the last minute, broke off treatment for months on end, and evinced an indifference and implicit hostility to the treatment. Over a period of years, however, he began to realize that my stance of

acceptance and inquiry threatened his image of himself as one having grown up in a happy family, as one whose primary difficulties
stemmed from not knowing "what to do" about various difficulties
in his life; he said he felt ashamed that he should feel so hateful
toward an attitude of tolerance. This patient sought some measure of
reassurance in his wish that I agree with him in condemning his sexual inhibitions and his difficulties with sexual orientation. By contrast, an attitude of tolerance toward the source of his shame produced anxiety and confusion.

SIZE SYMBOLISM AND FANTASIZED MEASUREMENT

Size symbolism brings the infant into a universe of comparisons,
essential to an understanding of the world. Because others are either
larger or smaller than oneself, in any two-person relationship one
person or the other will be used as the measure of height, whether
"taller," or "smaller." What matters is not who is objectively taller
or smaller, but rather whose size is experienced to be the standard by
which the other is measured. In all relationships, it would seem,
experienced size is relationship oriented, and fluctuates depending
upon perceptions of strength or importance. Franz Kafka wrote in
the 1919 "Letter to His Father" of a memory of being "a little skele-
ton" undressing with his father. "There I was, skinny, weakly, slight;
you strong, tall, broad. Even inside the hut I felt a miserable specimen, and what's more, not only in your eyes but in the eyes of the
whole world, for you were for me the measure of all things."[26] In
relation to his father Kafka developed "an impression of helpless singularity, of being a 'slave living under laws invented only for him.' A
shame literally unspeakable attached itself to this impression." And,
as John Updike comments, one of the forces driving Kafka to write
was shame over this "helpless singularity," shame over not being
able to connect with his father in a mode that was not persecutory.[27]

Clearly it is undesirable for the analyst to harbor unanalyzed fantasies that he or she is the standard of measurement, since such assumptions forestall the feelings of competition in the patient, and constitute
a recipe for mutual blindness. Patients (and analysts) wishing unconsciously to avoid comparison and competition will attempt to "hide"
their shame and vulnerability by avoiding situations in which competitive strivings might (either in fantasy or in reality) be detected.

Like Alice, we can feel large or small with respect both to our inner evaluations, and to those we perceive and/or imagine others judge us by. When these feel as unstable as they do to Alice, the universe appears absurd, surreal, and nonsensical. Either it becomes impossible to take evaluations or criticism from outsiders seriously, or one wants simply to snuff out the one who looks. You will recall that the Lilliputians wished to put Gulliver's eyes out, so they would no longer feel he dwarfed them. Once blinded, he could not see what they did not wish him to perceive and what they did not wish to perceive in themselves. But Gulliver discovers that the Brobdingnagians too could be made to feel uncomfortable under his gaze, however small he is when compared to them. While discussing politics, one of the ministers "observed how contemptible a thing was human grandeur, which could be mimicked by such diminutive insects as I."[28]

Envy plays an important role in defending against the shame of defect: rather than feel that it is oneself who is lacking something, one can feel envious of some *other* person who has what one does not (and can by projection be contemptuous of oneself in one's stead). In this way, various forms of envy and contempt can be covers for shame, sometimes by reversal; it is not *I* who is ashamed but *you* who are contemptuous; it is not *I* who am lacking but *you* who have what I want.

Paul Schilder, C. D. van der Velde, and others have stressed that human beings cannot form one complete image of the body. "Our bodily perceptions result in a multitude of different, independently established body images"[29] all, as it were, vying for the unattainable status of completion. Because our own ever-fluctuating judgments—and those of others—intervene in our assessments of our bodies, whatever we call "body image" is necessarily at variance with experienced body feelings. This means that we all use our body images dialectically: to control the way we feel about ourselves and to control the way we perceive others feel about us.

SIZE ANXIETY AND OEDIPAL SHAME: CLINICAL VARIANTS

Several clinical vignettes and patient dreams illustrate ways in which differences in size (both psychic and literal) communicate feelings about bodies, relationships, and internal states.

The first patient is Sam, a man in his late forties, small in stature. I am tall (6'3") whereas this patient is short (roughly 5'6"). Throughout the analysis (and in the transference) he feels he has had to come up against "big powerful people" who represent his narcissistic, powerful father who was an internationally prominent man in his field. Born during the war, he lived alone with his mother as "the man of the house" for the first several years of his existence, until his father and brother returned home when he was about three. In his struggles with such "powerful men," he feels he has habitually come up short, and not only is humiliated but will be more humiliated if he lets on how humiliated he feels.

Sam dreams:

> I was standing in a railroad station. There were trains going past every which way. I had to cross over to another platform to get to my train. I only wanted to go a little way. Mine was a local train. The station was very large with lots of trains, express trains. There were so many trains going in and out. It was all very confusing. I felt some sense of urgency about getting my little train. Because the journey I wanted to make was a very small one, I could not find my train. Just as I was about to get to my small train, this very fast train came in. It was not stopping at this station. It was enormous and going very fast. A very long train. It kept on going on as though it would never end. I was confused and frustrated at having to wait.

Sam's associations led him to speak of having to wait for me earlier in the week, of his confusion and frustration at having others ("larger" people with "larger agendas") keep him waiting, and of the humiliation he feels if he lets anyone know how upset he is when kept waiting. He went on to express his anxieties that I would not have room for him in my agenda, since he was "too small," and that he could not let me know how much he resented my sense of my own importance, since that made him seem envious and feel lacking. Although he tried to scale down his ambitions, in fantasy Sam's ambitions were very large indeed, so that with respect to them his achievements were forever being diminished.

Sam commented that often in his dreams there is an atmosphere of a large, immense space with diminutive people huddled in corners. Another dream: "I am trying to cross a street. It is a busy street. I get down on my knees and am crossing the street when an enormous bus nearly runs into me. When I get to the other side, I stand up and look around. But nobody has noticed me at all."

A third, typically Oedipal dream expressed Sam's feeling that he *has* to be small, since there is no room for him.

> I am in my parents' bed. My father is taking up a great deal of room, but my mother urges me to come next to her, where there is a small space. I go there, and then feel my father disapproving. I go outside and walk around for a while, and then return. This time my father is taking up more of the bed. There is no room at all for me. Thinking I have nowhere to go and that the dream has nowhere to go, I awake.

Feelings of smallness can thus be linked to actual size in the analytic situation. Sam experienced his smallness by comparison to me, making me very large, a confirmation in fantasy of his feelings of insignificance; having been and being continually overlooked and diminished all his life, here he is being diminished once again. Sam's struggles to assert his own importance run into Oedipal obstacles; if he feels large, he feels dangerous. To control his rage and dangerousness, he relies on others to "put him down," as in this last dream in which he feels that room for him in the bed is taken up by his father, and he has nowhere to go. He "belittles" himself continually, both as an expression of helplessness and as a defense against the rage he feels toward his father and other "large men" (like myself) who deprive him even of small spaces, who stand in his way and push him out.[30]

Not surprisingly for one who had to rely on others to keep him down and to feel small in order to keep his rage under control, Sam was fascinated with spies; they always worked with tiny instruments that could be planted without chance of detection. "They don't want big things, " he explained to me. "Since the whole point is not to be seen doing what you are doing, you work with miniatures; you love tiny things: tiny cameras that unseen can photograph things."

Sometimes magnifying persons in dreams can represent a dilution of the dreamer, like looking through the wrong end of a telescope. Frederico Fellini, whose films rely heavily upon dreams, and who once commented that "reality distorts," wrote of Anita Ekberg that she inspired in him "the incredulity one has before creatures of exceptional height, like the giraffe or the elephant."[31] When size anxiety and shame become too intense, the environment becomes so plastic that the contours of the person disappear. This is what happens in *Alice.* Just as healthy narcissism can be associated with a stability in what I have termed *psychic size,* so pathological narcissism (and pathological shame) may be related to an instability in psychic size.

> The recognition and assertion of one's own self as genuinely existing, a valuable entity of a given size, shape and significance—is attainable only when the positive interest of the environment . . . guarantees the stability of that form of personality by means of external pressure, so to speak. Without such a counter-pressure, let us say counter-love, the individual tends to explode, to dissolve itself in the universe, perhaps to die.[32]

Experienced disruption in the "counter-love" can also be understood as a loss of poise, a state of imbalance and accompanying feelings of awkwardness. Leo Rangell (1954) has explained poise as a state of equilibrium between forces,

> the quality of expected stimulus and the sum of the ego resources ready to meet it. The two are poised in equal balance and there is momentarily a suspension of motion.[33]

To summarize, Sam's experience of being small in my presence communicates a feeling of unpreparedness (and hence anxiety), of not being up to the task of coming up against me or I against him, feelings that represent his fear of his own explosive impulses and rage and may be directly related to Oedipal shame.[34]

THE SHAPE OF EXPERIENCE AND FANTASIES OF SIZE

Believing oneself to be large or small can express both feelings of helplessness and humiliation (being too small to be considered or too conspicuous to fit in) and feelings of rage, rivalry, and danger (endangering others). Without an experience of "counter-love," the experience of some important person whose love pushes back, the self is in danger of falling apart or exploding, a danger in response to which magical (and compensatory) fantasies can be summoned to shrink competitors, like the heads of the enemies of the Jivaro, a South American tribe known for boiling the heads of their enemies until they are a fraction of their normal volume. Enemies are thus "reduced" to compensate for what is experienced to be their dangerous importance, since they threaten one's needed appearance; one does away with the competition by shrinking it.

Dreams of shrinking and fantasies of disappearance can also represent feelings of distance from the analyst, expressing the re-living, re-membering, and re-cognition in the analytic situation of experiences of remoteness from parents during childhood. People who are far away *do* look smaller, as those who are up close *do* look larger, and can therefore express feelings of emotional closeness and remoteness. Yet, as in the case of Thurber's Walter Mitty, however painful the grim realities of humdrum existence, too great a reliance upon a fantasy world points up one's underlying impotence in the face of "reality," and therefore must inevitably remain a potential source of shame, as Carroll's poem *My Fancy* reminds us.

> I painted her a gushing thing,
> With years perhaps a score;
> I little thought to find they were
> At least a dozen more;
> My fancy gave her eyes of blue,
> A curly auburn head;
> I came to find the blue a green,
> The auburn turned to red.
>
> She boxed my ears this morning,
> They tingled very much;
> I wish that I would wish her
> A somewhat lighter touch;
> And if you were to ask me how
> Her charms might be improved,
> I would not have them *added to,*
> But just a *few removed!*
>
> She has the bear's ethereal grace,
> The bland hyena's laugh,
> The footstep of the elephant,
> The neck of the giraffe;
> I love her still, believe me,
> Though my heart its passion hides;
> "She's all my fancy painted her,"
> But oh! *how much besides.*

In *Alice,* Carroll uses the metaphor of the telescope to describe sensations of both shrinking and opening up. In a stroke of genius, he relies upon nonsense to protect Alice from her identity confusion so that she can more freely imagine who she is in contradistinction to the bizarre and "not-her" creatures of Wonderland. But Alice's instability in size only points up a basic theme in Carroll's work: there can be no imagined appearance that can ever be adequate, which can provide in fantasy an antidote to feeling so bested by the Queen, so misperceived, alone, and lost. If we can only know who we are, what size we are, how we look, and so forth by imagining how others see us, *and* we experience from others intractable non-recognition, we find ourselves caught in a tragic situation and endless struggle the outcome of which is always uncertain. This is the world of Luigi Pirandello, to which we will now turn.

2 Fantasy, Anguish, and Misconstrual

And by this time, even for her, her voice no longer issued
from her own lips, but from those he imagined she had;
and if she laughed, she suddenly had the impression of not
having laughed herself, but rather of having imitated a
smile that was not hers, the smile of that other self who
lived within his mind.

—Luigi Pirandello, *Una Voce*

PIRANDELLO AND THE UNRECOGNIZABLE

The Sicilian author Luigi Pirandello, not wanting his dead body
exposed to the gaze of the public, gave the following written instruc-
tions concerning its disposal: "When I am dead, do not clothe me.
Wrap me naked in a sheet. No flowers on the bed and no lighted can-
dle. A pauper's cart. And let no one accompany me, neither relatives
nor friends. The cart, the horse, the coachman *e basta*. Burn
me. . . ."[1]

Of modern writers, none have wrestled with fears of being
unrecognizable, looking in vain, and needing to hide—with the modern tragedy of appearance and shame—more powerfully than has
Pirandello. As the Father in his play *Six Characters in Search of an
Author* observes, even when we manage to "clothe ourselves in outward dignity," inwardly each one of us is "lots and lots of people. . . .
The person you are with me is quite different from the person you
are with somebody else." There are shameful and "unconfessable

25

intimate things that go on." This unknowable yet stoutly defended intimacy acquires great power. Over and over again Pirandello characters attempt to "keep up" appearances, to struggle in vain "to reestablish the old dignity, set it upright whole and solid, like a tombstone over a grave." As Pirandello notes, "That way we don't have to look at our shame."[2]

Not only is keeping up appearances utterly vain, but worse, the very attempts to do so contribute to one's undoing. Pained at having themselves represented by actors who do not and cannot know them and who do not even look like them, the Six Characters protest at their "realization"[3] in the hands of others. "This is what we look like. You can see these are *our* bodies, these are *our* faces. . . ."[4] To which the Producer admonishes, "There is no place here for you, as yourself. Here you just don't exist. An actor represents you, that's all," an idea picked up with despair by the Father, who believes that any attempt on his part to communicate will be subverted by the actors. No actor can be "me, as I feel myself to be inside here," he cries, a sentiment echoed by his Son. "Your actors can only look at us from the outside! How can you expect anybody to live their life in front of a kind of distorting mirror, which doesn't just freeze our expressions in a reflected image, but twists it into a total travesty we don't even recognize?"[5]

The unsuccessful struggle to get the world to give back a tolerable likeness traverses all of Pirandello's work, and expresses a deep sense of internal instability.[6] Small wonder, then, that his characters make futile but ever greater efforts to stabilize appearances. Feeling unrecognizable to themselves, Pirandello's characters look to others, and in that reliance lies frustration, rage, torment, and despair. Gripped by shame conflicts and by fears of being bested, humiliated, and abandoned, Pirandello's anguished characters struggle to be recognized in the face of those who cannot see.

Again and again in my work with my patients, I come up against their overpowering feeling that they are unrecognizable, that there is no place for them as themselves, that consequently they are struggling against both fears of recognition and fears of being not-seen. As they understand their relation to me in the transference, they repeat the sense of being doomed to be invisible while longing for recognition. They have great difficulty verbalizing these feelings, which seem to be so contradictory, so painful, so confusing, so humiliating, and so intimate.

As a reaction to the discrepancy between the way one fears one will be seen and the way one wants to appear, shame refers to imaginary (although sometimes shared) standards of self-evaluation (ego-ideals). Those who find that they cannot imagine themselves in the eyes of others rely ever more compulsively on their appearance in a vain effort to make themselves intelligible, an awareness of which leads to extraordinary vulnerability. A friend of Franz Kafka's wrote, "Frank cannot live. . . . He possesses not the slightest refuge. For that reason he is exposed to all those things against which we are protected. He is like a naked man among the multitude who are dressed,"[7] an idea that I will take up in my discussion of Pirandello's "Clothe the Naked."

Many writers and artists have spoken of their wish to disappear, to be anonymous. Rainer Maria Rilke born in 1875 in Prague, eight years older than Pirandello, wrote of fantasies of anonymity. "How blissful to wake in a place where no one expects you. . . . Oh, how that increased the lightness of my soul. . . ." Like his fictional character Malte,[8] Rilke wishes to be "nobody's son" and in his epitaph he yearns to be "nobody's sleep."[9] Similarly Charles Dickens, whose childhood abandonment is well documented and finds its way into his finest novels, wrote of himself, "What a blank space I seemed, which everybody overlooked, and yet was in everybody's way."[10]

SHAME AND OEDIPAL DEFEAT IN THE ANALYSIS OF SAM

Sam, whose dreams I discussed in the preceding chapter, was, as you will remember, the second of two sons born during the war. He grew up knowing his mother had sent his elder brother to another continent, saying he was "just a bundle," an ominous remark in the context of her having rid herself so easily of a cumbersome child. While his parents had always said that his elder brother had been sent abroad for his own safety, it gradually became clear to Sam that at the time there was, in fact, far more risk in sending the infant abroad than in keeping him at home.

You will also recall that Sam's father was well-known and brooked no competition. From his childhood, Sam was crippled by Oedipal shame. During his adult life, each time he was visibly successful, events and people would thwart him and reduce him to submission in the most humiliating ways. As the analysis progressed it became clear that Sam feared that if he became successful either financially or professionally, I would either punish or leave him (i.e., he would suffer a terrible and humiliating defeat). For example, in speaking of his decision to relocate his office, Sam realized that he was frightened and inhibited by his feelings of impotence.

> I may want to move, but I need something to happen, the rats or the noise, but it has to *seem* external. I have to manipulate things so it never seems as though I am the one doing something. A few people plan their lives, but not me. Every time I make a decision, it's disastrous. I run away at exactly the wrong point. If I've made decisions, they are wrong. . . . I am like people who get into fights to get beaten up, who engineer the situation. I can remember being so angry that I punish myself by creating a situation where someone else punishes me, and pushes me out. But I do everything with smoke and mirrors, yet I retain a sense of omnipotence and believe really I'm controlling it all, but I can never let on.

Here the sense of Oedipal defeat is monumental, yet it has been buried beneath shame and fantasies of omnipotence. Furthermore, the omnipotence makes the actual defeats and losses that much more unbearable. Consequently, Sam cannot feel "together."

> I can't be direct and say, "I want to stop the analysis now." But I suppose I'm as anxious about finishing the analysis as I am about finishing anything. I am anxious about seeing that all these things are *me*. While they are all separate, I can be invisible. But once it comes together, I am terrified people will see and say: "Now I can see what you are up to." To put myself together fills me with guilt. With you I can't say, "I think the analysis has gone as far as it can." I am so conscious of my tendency to evade and never confront things head on. Everything is more painful now that I can see it as it's happening. The analysis has made it so much more difficult for me to avoid feeling what I am doing. Watching myself, catching myself in the middle, I go crazy.

When appearance is shown to be vain, the wish to appear a certain way easily backfires, and becomes yet another shameful and humiliating defeat, or a shameful expression of rage, as is the case in the world of Pirandello. Sam explains with reference to a Christmas card how anonymous and without attachment he feels, how incapable of responding even to himself.

> I got a Christmas card dated November 18. It was sent to the old P. O. box. I opened it up, but there was no writing, no way of knowing who sent it. That upset me. I had the feeling that whoever sends the card expects me to respond. However, I can't respond since I don't know who to send it to.

Sam has picked up on a theme of not being able to bring his father, himself, or indeed, anyone, into his sights, which lends an understandably insubstantial, vacuous cast to all his relationships. I suggest to him that in the analysis (as well as in his professional and family life) he is reluctant to have himself recognized, that with everyone he does something analogous to sending a card without signing it. And I add that he seems reluctant to give me something essential of himself to respond to. In response to this interpretation he comments,

> I imagine being a spy who works unseen, creating things that will change the world. The unseen is so fascinating to me. The star depends on being known and the spy on not being known. I fantasize about being both, having a double identity. But being known in and of itself has no excitement, no wattage, for me.

Sam avoided conflicts with his father by using shame and appearance anxiety to come out always the small one, the one who was bested. His father was larger than life, and the one everybody knew and admired. Sam, by contrast, always lost out. He grew up being recognized only as his father's son. Yet as an adult and in a position of professional prominence, Sam proved equally uncomfortable being recognized publically as accomplished since it triggered his consciousness of Oedipal struggles. When he felt threatening or felt that others experienced him as such, he retreated to a kind of zero degree of existence: he became no more than a placeholder who could make someone else's number intelligible. In that way his father and other Oedipal rivals could be protected against his rage, and Sam could protect himself against the shame of fearing he would once again be bested and humiliated.

Another session picks up on the difficulties he has with all relationships, in part because he feels he does not have what it takes to
feed any of them.

> What I was thinking on the way here was where we left off yes-
> terday. It is so difficult for me to keep in touch with people, with
> you. So many people have fallen by the wayside, just gone, dis-
> appeared. I can't keep in touch with anyone. It's all very unset-
> tling, how I cannot keep any connection. I am wondering why
> that is. It comes back to my father. I never went through any
> grieving when he died. There were three funeral services: one in
> New England, one in New York, and the memorial. At the first
> there wasn't any coffin because it had been sent to New York.
> Didn't feel much in New York, saw the coffin being put in [the]
> ground. Lots of people. I remember feeling alone. In New Eng-
> land I felt a tinge of sadness, then it sort of went. There is a sense
> I could never grieve.[11] There is no one I can think of with affec-
> tion.

Not only are Sam's relationships unstable, since he feels he can
do nothing active to maintain them, but he withholds affection and,
more fundamentally, withholds something of his own reality in retal-
iatory fashion: to punish his absent father, he withdraws. Consciously he realizes how angry he is with his father for not being
there and for sacrificing his children for the glory of his career. Yet
instead of blaming him, Sam is consumed by a sense of incapacitat-
ing guilt and envy; he finds himself lost in details, unable to make
headway with what he intends, and fundamentally ineffective in
imagining a future for himself. Such an inability produces a crushing
sense of defeat; in defense he omnipotently turns his father into a
specter in whose eyes, by definition, he can never be a worthy oppo-
nent. Consequently, Sam's Oedipal struggles bog down in cycles of
crippling shame, envy, humiliation and defeat, murderous rage, and
incalculable sadness.

> If I lost my little daughter or my wife, there is a physicality
> which I would have to remember them by. A voice or smile
> would stay. Missing that makes you sad. But with my father,
> nothing jumps out in an affectionate way. If I cough, I feel I've
> heard him cough like that, but the memory does not come with
> any sense of affection at all. When he would come to school to
> visit me, he seemed to do it out of obligation. He never did any-

thing I can think of so that I can remember him in a way I can feel. I don't remember. I remember his lying on the beach and carving a bit of granite. He was one of the most remote people imaginable. And he enjoyed belittling me. So I don't feel sad he's gone, since there was nothing about him which endeared him in any way. He was a most unintimate, cold, distant, and rather vicious person. What made him happy was when the attention was turned on him or people laughed at his jokes.

Having expressed his feeling of how very remote his father was, and how much he longed for contact with him, he then proceeded to speak about his shame-ridden inhibitions in expressing his needs to me or anyone.

I feel sad now that the only way I could know him was to idealize him as a great man . . . I'm trying to link this up with why I can't keep in touch with people. . . . There is a sense I don't need people. I don't need anyone; I can manage without; there is no one in my life who can make any significant difference. Sometimes when I call you I feel you don't want to talk. That's the connection: losing things; I don't feel I need them. Same with relationships. Nice to have met you but if I never see you again, it doesn't matter; in fact it's better. That way there's no sadness or loss.

Behind the idealization is shame and sadness, and a profound sense of anger, isolation, and loss that can be defended against by disconnecting. But the shame of profound loss is made all the more intolerable by Sam's sense that there is nothing at all to hold onto, no way of fixing memories to feelings: they just disappear along with the people they represent. And since he feels no abiding connection with anyone, he too is in constant danger of disappearing. Whether his objects disappear or he disappears, the result is the same. If he cannot feel attachment to people, if he cannot feel something to remember them by, he cannot feel himself to be real and valuable. His growing awareness of this as a deep sense of shame was one of the hallmarks of his analysis. He continues:

I just cut myself off from work and from people. I keep this distance and never connect in the first place. If I choose to disconnect, I can do so easily. Even with my friend D, for a time I needed him and he needed me. Then poof, he was gone. . . . Yet by cutting people and things off I never have any sense of history, growth or development. I'm living in *this* moment *now*. Every day I'm reinvented; I've got no past, no future. If I'm getting on badly with my wife, I feel "I don't need this." And even though I know she loves me, unless I see it in front of my eyes, I don't believe it. If we have a fight, I can't believe she loves me. One bad day and I feel I'm finished. Everything has this finality and immediacy. One bad day at work and I feel I'm bad, and will never do anything good again. I'm out and disconnected.[12]

Some months later he returned to the theme of how painful it is for him to feel his identity in constant flux.

It's a matter of identity. You must identify with the person you're connecting with. You have to see something in you that you see in them. Every relationship has some form of identification. I want to see similarity. What is so painful for me is that I rarely find it.[13] *You could say that you are without an identity when you can't recognize in others what you can't see in yourself. Without an identity you can't make a connection.* All people I feel disconnected from. Like my father who said he felt no connection with the national tradition. *You feel disconnection the closer you get.*

Here, as he realizes the pain of getting closer to me, Sam puts together his difficulties connecting (object relations) with his own narcissism, which prevents his being able to see something recognizable in others. Unless he feels something recognizable in others, he cannot feel they can feel anything recognizable in himself, which leads to profound feelings of alienation and despair.

In the final phase of the analysis, Sam recognizes that, as illogical as it might seem, behind the experience of being different people and of disappearing lie his own fantasies of omnipotence that people (his analyst) can see. And he is afraid that these omnipotence fantasies will be seen to make a mockery of his obstacles and of his efforts to overcome them, another hallmark of Oedipal shame.

Like Sam, Pirandello feels that he's different people. In *Six Characters*, the "imaginary" author cannot get his characters to communicate what he wants them to; the characters cannot express themselves because they are dependent upon the actors; the actors have their own preoccupations and disagreements, and are prevented from doing their jobs because of interference from the characters.[14]

Doubts about identity intensify the dependency on others for some reassuring definition, for an adequate "role." Yet such dependency is doomed to failure, since it inevitably leads to distortions in both oneself and others, to a "hiding to nothing," a British phrase that seems so well suited to experiences of vanishing. It also fuels attempts to gain control over the way one feels oneself to be seen. Otto Fenichel noted that "'I feel ashamed' means 'I do not want to be seen,'" and that shame and not looking go together. And he added that gaze aversion can be a "kind of magical gesture, arising from the magical belief that anyone who does not look cannot be looked at."[15] The more ashamed one is, the more ipso facto one depends on one's experiences of others' looking, no matter how painful.[16]

THE HEARTBREAKING CURIOSITY OF THE BLIND

What Sam says about his impulse to disconnect, to disappear out of unbearable shame, can be felt in one of Pirandello's remarkable early short stories, "Una Voce" ("A voice") in which Pirandello probes the subject of appearance, misconstrual and human tragedy through the motif of physical blindness. Shortly before her death, the Marchesa Borghi decides to consult the great ophthalmologist, Dr. Giunio Falci, about the blindness of her son Silvio, diagnosed with incurable glaucoma. Within the first page, it is clear that all of the characters are deluded in one way or another. None can see clearly. Only Dr. Falci is lucid. But his lucidity comes at a great cost.

> He [Dr. Falci] had gradually formed a concept of life so devoid of all those friendly and almost necessary hypocrisies, those spontaneous, inevitable illusions composed and created by each one of us without our volition, through an instinctive need—for social decency, one might say—that his company had now become intolerable.[17]

Dr. Falci examines Silvio and concludes that he can do nothing. Then the Marchesa dies.[18] In part as a response to the void and darkness of his mother's death, Silvio becomes curious about Lydia, the woman to whose care he has been entrusted by his mother. "Soon, with the timid but obstinate and heartbreaking curiosity of the blind" he began questioning her. In response to his questions, she began to "make every effort to resemble that fictitious image he had of her, every effort to see herself the way he saw her in his darkness." Her sense of herself began to change; "even for her, her voice no longer issued from her own lips, but from those he imagined she had."[19]

The two become increasingly involved the one with the other. Some time thereafter, Dr. Falci reconsiders his diagnosis and, without knowing she has died, returns to the Marchesa's house. He is greeted by the wary and possessive Lydia, now Silvio's fiancée and soon-to-be wife. She suggests he come back after the wedding. At Dr. Falci's insistence, Lydia reluctantly goes to get Silvio, to whom it is explained that Dr. Falci may be able to cure him. In the presence of Dr. Falci, Lydia mentions to Silvio that the doctor had come to the house on the very day of the Marchesa's death, but she turned him away. Sensing some impossible disjunction between herself and Silvio, Lydia struggles with the decision to try Dr. Falci's operation. Before going to the clinic, Silvio realizes that "her tears were not the same as his." All during the day before he was to go for the operation, she "intoxicated him with that voice of hers, self-assured because he was still there, in his darkness."[20] The day before he is to return from the clinic, his eyesight restored, Lydia gathers her possessions and departs.

The story demonstrates powerfully how reliant Lydia is on what Silvio cannot see: she can invent herself only through his unseeing eyes. She has to become—and remain—the voice through which he imagines her. Similarly, Sam harbored a fantasy that he could feel whole only if I did not see how many disparate parts and pieces of him there were. Consequently, he depended on my blindness (as on the blindness of others) to feel tolerable to himself. As a result, however, he felt overlooked, slighted, not recognized, and cut off. Little by little I came to see that I could be ashamed of what I didn't see in him, and, indeed, that such shame was an indispensable part of the analytic process. As I came to better tolerate my shame at being blind to parts of him, he began to tolerate his shame more easily.

If a patient feels that he has lost control over the way he appears, he can attempt to wrestle it back by imposing his fantasy-construction on the one who looks (e.g., the analyst). Lydia, for instance, has lost control over the way she appears. She is, as it were, moored externally, and therefore must reinvent the mooring in order not to feel so much at the mercy of those around her. But such fantasized defenses cannot alter either her deeply injured sense of pride (the narcissistic wound) or her hermetically sealed ideals of who she feels she must but cannot be (her ego ideal). In listening to our patients, we as analysts, through them, listen to our own voices, and wonder how blind they need to be to us, how blind they need us to be to them. When successful, the analytic enterprise can undo blindness (in patients and analysts), and provide encouragement and strength in tolerating—and transforming—shame and anxiety.

3 A Hole in a Paper Sky

Deceit and Remedies by Still More Deceit

> Suppose that, at the climax, when the marionette who is
> playing Orestes is about to avenge his father's death and
> kill his mother and Aegisthus, a little hole were torn in the
> paper sky above him? Orestes would still want his
> revenge, yet when he saw that hole, he would feel helpless.
> Orestes would become Hamlet! That's the difference
> between ancient tragedy and modern: a hole in a paper
> sky.
>
> —Pirandello, *The Late Mattia Pascal*

Whereas in Greek tragedy in general and Sophocles in particular,
matters of identity may be related to cultural ideals organized, at
least in part, around relatively nonproblematic notions of honor,[1]
beyond the heavens of contemporary tragedy lies a void continually
threatening to show through: there is no stable ideal on which to rely
for protection. The Greeks acknowledged the importance of social
ideals and reputation (e.g., *The Iliad*), which constituted a shared
defense against shame; in ancient Greece organizing ideals like honor
made the universe seem intelligible. And there was an investment in
maintaining collective illusions about the nature of this social and
conceptual order.[2] By contrast, for us there are gaping holes in the
fabric of any imaginable order.[3] In our contemporary world public
figures have difficulty defending their private lives.[4]

In Luigi Pirandello's image of Orestes put on by marionettes, when Orestes is about to kill his mother, a small hole appears in the paper sky above him, a "hole in a paper sky."[5] Orestes cannot go through with murdering his mother.

> Still the thought of the puppet Orestes, disturbed by a hole in the sky, lingered for a long time in my mind,—lucky marionettes, I sighed, over whose wooden heads the false sky has no holes! No anguish or perplexity, no hesitations, obstacles, shadows, pity— nothing! And they can go right on with their play and enjoy it, they can love, they can respect themselves, never suffering from dizziness or fainting fits, because for their stature and their actions that sky is a proportionate roof.[6]

Overcome by indecision and inaction, Orestes becomes Hamlet. The tragic virtues of honor, pride, and harmony so essential for the Greek theater, give way in our contemporary world to off-kilter shams and misguided attempts to seem intelligible.

SHAME AND AIDOS

Let us now turn briefly to the Greek concept of *aidos*, the Greek word that we translate as "shame" and that also designates the genitalia. Shame appears in the Greek world as an experience of "being seen, inappropriately, by the wrong people, in the wrong condition."[7] Shamed individuals struggle to regain their honor, failing which they are driven to suicide. In the "Ajax" of Sophocles, Ajax kills himself out of shame. As Bernard Williams writes, "Being what he is, he could not live as the man who had done these things (slaying sheep instead of men because he is tricked into so doing by Athena); it is impossible, in virtue of the relations between what he expects of the world and what the world expects of a man who expects that of it."[8]

When the gods went to laugh at the spectacle of Aphrodite and Ares caught inextricably *in flagrente delicto* by Haephestos' nets, the goddesses stayed at home, *aidoi*, "from shame." Using the word *aidos*, Homer describes Nausikaa's embarrassment at the idea of mentioning to her father her desire for marriage, Penelope's refusal to appear by herself before the suitors, and Thetis' hesitation to go and visit the gods. Similarly, Odysseus is embarrassed or ashamed that the Phaiakians should see him crying; Isocrates says that in the old days if young men had to cross the agora, they did so, "with great shame and embarrassment."[9] In *The Iliad*, shame-prone and honor-seeking Hector feared criticism by someone of inferior status, but his fear of such people made him feel that much more ashamed.

SHAME AND THE SNEEZE: THE ANALYSIS OF MARK

Social theoriests have for centuries contrasted the social emotions (e.g., shame) with the individual emotions (e.g., guilt and egoism). Sociologists (e.g., Scheff and Retzinger, 1991; and Tisseron, 1992) have emphasized how "social" an emotion is the shame of being excluded, and how powerful a driving force ostracism can be.

Speaking in his analysis about the feeling that he has been pushed out all his life, Mark muses about what they say in Hollywood. "'You'll never have lunch in this town again.' You're out. Happened to me again and again. He makes our life difficult. We will punish him by ignoring him, rejecting him and banishing him." And then Mark sneezes.

What does the sneeze express and how can it be understood? In this case, the sneeze expresses a conflict between, on the one hand, the feeling of humiliation at having been pushed out, and, on the other, the anger which, by projection, Mark attributes to those who push him out because he is threatening (i.e., powerful). He feels his conflicts over potency and power to be too dangerous to be held: they must be expelled so that they can be gotten rid of before they become conscious.

> I sneezed because I really *could* do that and it *would* make my mother happy. What holds me back is the anger. It is relevant to what you called the "crimp" in my imagination. Something gets stuck in my craw. There is too much anger. Anger at having things taken away from me. Is it real or is it some screwed up way of seeing things, this feeling that things have always been taken away from me?

In asking the question he is reflecting upon a pattern of feelings the meanings of which he has not previously been free to consider. If other people are not necessarily powerful, bad, and responsible for his feeling of being pushed out, then he is uncertain about their reality, and, by extension, about himself.

I feel that I'm bad, and that I have to punish the part that is bad by not having anything at all to do with it. My wife said I don't really know who I am. She's right. This bad person I don't want anything to do with. All parts of me are all split up and separate. I am like the ringmaster at the circus with a whip trying to keep these parts under control. All fighting among themselves. I try to have all these personalities cowering on their knees, too terrified to do anything. That's a good analogy. There is this huge lion which could easily, oh so easily, kill the ringmaster.

Realizing that I may be the ringmaster in fantasy, I point out that he may feel no single part of him can have dominion over the others without tyranny, that he relies on the terror and the subjugation (i.e., the whip) of the circus master, on powerful figures like his father to keep the discrepant parts in line, an intervention to which he responds by speaking about his different parts.

There is this incredible separation in me all the time. It makes people suspicious. Maybe not you. Can never tell. Never know which one of my personalities is going to be the problem today: sometimes I feel angry, hopeless, depressed, self-defeating, horribly sensitive, an incompetent mess, can't do anything. And at other times I think I can do anything, that I have incredible powers.

Having articulated a sense of omnipotence, Mark becomes noticeably anxious. "I am terrified that the control is not real. But it is *real* to me. To you, it might seem pathetic or crazy." The omnipotent control *has* to be real to him; otherwise he is hopelessly bogged down in shame, rage, and anxiety. Whether the omnipotence fantasies constitute a reaction to the shame and humiliation he feels, or whether the shame comes in part from the discrepancies between omnipotence fantasies and paltry reality does not really matter, since they feed on each other. The clinical focus, I think, needs to be the patient's difficulty in knowing what is real and what is fantasy, and how shameful such a difficulty feels to him. In terms of Oedipal conflicts, if I challenge his sense of reality by attempting to explore his feelings of shame over not knowing what is real to him, this produces a crushing sense of Oedipal defeat. The task, then, is to allow him to feel the hole in the paper sky, so as better to grasp the illusion in his omnipotence and the reality of both his limitations and his possibilities.

DECEPTION, OUTRAGE, AND REMEDY BY EVER MORE DECEIT

Such uncertainty about what is real, such cycles of shame and fear of being thrown out, followed by rage and then guilt naturally contribute to attempted remedies by ever more encompassing deceit. To move from the individual conflicts of Mark back to Pirandello and to the social world, it is pertinent to recall the structure of Pirandello's plays: a "center of suffering and a periphery of busybodies—the pattern of a Sicilian village."[10] A drama of suffering unfolds before a crowd of Sicilian villagers (doubled, of course, by us as members of the audience), engendering noxious shame, organized around fears of being shut out and isolated, in response to which there is "deception, outrage, and remedy by larger deceit."[11]

In Pirandello's "Right You Are If You Think You Are" (both story and play), the Sicilian townsfolk are told first by Signora Frola that her son-in-law is crazy and delusional, and then told by the son-in-law, Signor Ponza, that his mother-in-law is completely round the bend. It becomes impossible for the townsfolk to know which one is telling the truth. Readers, viewers, and townsfolk alike know so little about either Frola or Ponza that they are forced to see each through the eyes of the other. Each onlooker has a different set of perceptions; each imagines himself in the eyes of the others to whom he can be "different people." Given, then, this profusion of imagined appearances, it is impossible to establish objective truth and have it mean much at all.[12]

Logically, of course, someone might suggest using town records to decide the matter. And indeed Laudisi does, but then immediately dismisses the idea. "Personally I don't give a rap for the documents; for the truth in my eyes is not in them but in the mind. . . ."[13] Moreover, the efforts of the townspeople to understand the claims of Frola and Ponza only lead to more frustration and confusion. Nobody can leave the matter open. All press compulsively for some kind of closure. Laudisi suggests that the missing person "is the phantom of the second wife, if Signora Frola is right. It's the phantom of the daughter, if Signor Ponza is right." And he adds, "It remains to be seen if what is a phantom for him and her is actually a person for herself," a remark that recalls the observations of Sam, to whom other people felt so insubstantial that he could not imagine how anyone could experience him as real.

When at the end of the Pirandello play the missing person actually appears in the person of Ponza, all expect the mystery can finally be solved.[14] Instead, she reaffirms the theme of the play: that she who is nobody to herself can be anybody at all—or nobody at all—to others. "I am the daughter of Signora Frola . . . and the second wife of Signor Ponza . . . and for myself, I am nobody . . . I am she whom you believe me to be."[15] By implication, then, the desire of the people in Valdana to believe both Ponza and Frola (each convinced the other was mad) lead to an impossible dilemma: neither can be demonstrated to be deceitful or delusional. The missing person, Signora Ponza, who is Nobody to herself, functions as the organizing principle of the play since she can be Anyone at all.

The power in the eyes (imagined and real) of the Sicilian villagers can deconstruct even the most stoutly defended sense of identity. As Pirandello observes,

> Pause for a moment and stare at someone who is performing the most ordinary and obvious act in life, stare at him in such a manner that what he is doing is not clear to us, and that it may similarly not be clear to himself; do this, and his self-assurance at once is overcast and begins to waiver. No crowd could be more disconcerting than that pair of unseeing eyes, eyes that do not see us, or which do not see the same thing that we do.[16]

The identity-shattering powers of the look, whether that of the characters or the villagers, can be escaped only by deception. And deception then constitutes a kind of willed disappearance from the gaze of the onlookers; one can only appear other than one is. Deception, outrage, and remedy by larger deceit was, it may be added, the pattern of President Nixon, who, like the characters in Pirandello, placed too much stake on appearance. "You've got to be always thinking in terms of the presidency, and the president should not appear to be hiding and not be forthcoming," he told the White House counsel John W. Dean III on March 16, 1973. As Nixon later acknowledged, it was the cover-up, rather than the Watergate acts, which drove him from the White House. And, ironically, it was Nixon's ideal of the presidency and of the president (who should not *appear* to be hiding) that sealed his fate as one who will be known for trying to cover up.[17] Seen in this light, recent attempts to impeach President Clinton call attention to cover-ups. Although there is also a compelling case to be made for an historical context of the Republican attacks on him going back ten or twenty years and having to do with American political culture, psychologically there is some basis for the public rage and determination not to let him off scot-free. Talk of "spin" and "spin doctors," and recent films like *Wag the Dog* underscore how little confidence we have in our abilities to see shams for what they are.[18] Events easily become a "transcendental farce" in which, as Pirandello comments, what the universe builds up it can as easily pull down, unable to take its own creations seriously.[19] This is the world of the so-called postmodernists.

"The necessity for mutual deception," Pirandello wrote in his essay on humor,

> is directly proportionate to the difficulty of the struggle for survival and to the person's awareness of his own weakness in this struggle. The pretense of strength, honor, sympathy, intelligence, in short of every virtue including the greatest, honesty, is a form of adaptation, a handy weapon in the struggle.[20]

And in two bitterly funny stories Pirandello depicts these identity conflicts. In "Puberty," a pubescent girl, perplexed by changes in her body, becomes surprised and horrified by her own odors. In the final scene, she is hysterically aroused by the sight of the white calves of her English tutor, who is sent from the house while she screams at him from the upstairs window to take her with him and then jumps to her death. In "Prudence" (Prudenza, 1901) the narrator, in his mid thirties, graying, out of sorts, and thoroughly disenchanted with his mistress, decides to go for a shave. The barber makes mistake after mistake, shaving both head and face, until the narrator can no longer recognize himself in the mirror. Furious, he storms home, only to discover his mistress cannot recognize him either and orders him out of the house, whereupon he finds himself a free man at last.[21]

THE VAIN INVENTION OF THE ONLOOKER

Such cycles of blindness and mutual deceit create ever more fervent and compulsive attempts to control appearances, which, in turn, lead to greater blindness generating still more anxiety, and, often, primitive rage. Suicidally enraged patients often describe Pirandellean feelings of being—like the Father in *Six Characters*—caught, suspended, and misshapen by their own powerlessness to imagine themselves in any way that would not be unbearable, enraged at what they feel is the power they give to others to define them by distortion. Such patients feel profoundly misunderstood, isolated, helpless to communicate something essential of who they are, and mortally ashamed of their predicament. When all else fails, one reinvents the onlooker.

Anguished deceit distinguishes our world fundamentally from the world of Sophocles. In Sophocles there are, if not gods, at least visions of honor in the heavens. And the sky, however bloody, is somehow solid. By contrast, in Pirandello and in our own world the entire construction is flimsy, the sky is paper, and there is a hole opening onto a wellspring of human helplessness.

4 What Do You See Me to Be?

Invisibility and Performance

I by no means think a single bad action condemns a man,
for he probably condemns it as much as you do; nor a single bad habit, for he is probably trying all his life to get rid
of it. A man is only thoroughly profligate when he has lost
the sense of right and wrong; or a thorough hypocrite,
when he has not even the wish to be what he appears.

—William Hazlitt

However appealing in theory, wishing to be no more than what one
appears to be can have a variety of diabolical outcomes. In this chapter I will be concerned with fantasies of invisibility and performance
anxiety, placing the two together because I think that the same
dynamics are at play in both.

Fantasies of invisibility express a wish, as well as a fear, not to
be seen or known. However, by putting himself beyond harm's reach,
he who relies on invisibility fantasies ipso facto isolates himself from
others, ostracizes himself, and reinforces his feelings of helplessness.
Whether one is no more than what one appears to be or no more
than what one disappears to be, the end result is the same: isolation.
Performers run great risks who rely too heavily on fantasies that they
are no more than they appear.

The Baconian tradition, which equates seeing with knowing,
assumes (following eighteenth-century Enlightenment ideas) that
not-seeing is simply ignorance and cannot be anything else. The

extraordinary contribution of Freud was to view blindness in terms of unconscious conflicts, a contribution all the more crucial because the war cry of empiricism since the seventeenth century has reflected our confidence in the experimental method, symbolized by telescope and microscope. According to such versions of empiricism, "objectivity" is dependent upon what can be replicated, upon what "anyone" can see (with the proper equipment).

By contrast, the psychoanalytic tradition gives a prominent place to motivated ignorance,[1] represented by fantasies of invisibility. This psychoanalytic approach is rooted in the Platonic tradition. For Socrates, we do not see if we do not understand *how* we see, a process unforgettably described by Plato in his allegory of the cave in *The Republic*. For Plato, no matter how sophisticated the instrument, just "looking" (taken to be an activity distinct from knowing how one sees) can never be satisfactory. An essential part of understanding how we see is understanding how and what we do not see, becoming aware of what blinds us and tolerating the shame of having been blind.

EXPOSURE AND INVISIBILITY: ADAM

From one vantage point, fantasies of invisibility provide a fantasized respite from fears of exposure. Carl Schneider[2] notes that our word "expose" is derived from the Latin *exponere*, a word that suggests an improper fit. People who feel "exposed" believe there is no place for them in the world; they are "put out," exiguous, ostracized, "out of the context within which they wish to be interpreted." To be exposed is thus to be seen without a context or in the wrong context. In response to fears of exposure, one may fantasize disappearing or, conversely, fantasize controlling the way one is seen, inventing in fantasy a context for others to see one in. In the first instance, we are dealing with defensive fantasies of invisibility; in the second, with defensive fantasies of exhibitionism. As we shall see, both are directly related to performance anxiety.

Fantasies of invisibility can backfire, however, since they tend to produce fears of disappearing in reality, which, in turn, can be defended against by *actually* feeling invisible (the defense is further fortified): then, in theory, there is nothing to disappear. Two unconscious fears have been solved in fantasy: on the one hand the fear of exposure is avoided, since nobody can see you; on the other hand, the fear of disappearing has been put to rest because you do not feel visible. Needless to say, these attempted solutions prove most unsatisfactory.

For instance, consider the plight of Adam, a painter in analysis who had difficulty choosing paintings for an exhibition. Making choices to him meant falsifying himself, creating an image of himself that other people would think they understood, while he went unnoticed; his agony over choices expressed his fear that by choosing one painting over another he would inadvertently make himself invisible by complying with the wishes of others (e.g., his parents) that he not be there. He could not imagine an exhibition of his works that would not lead to a sense of humiliating exposure; if he chose old work that had a certain coherence, then he could not identify with it, and it seemed hopelessly distant from what he imagined he could do; if he chose only new work, it would never be new enough, and even if it could be, he would be using it to contribute to misunderstanding him, since it would have no past, no context.

Adam felt he had no control over the way people read his paintings, a matter about which he felt all the more anxious because of his ambivalence about having his paintings seen at all. But rather than feel this ambivalence, Adam wished to have people see his work a certain way, to create the "right" context. The problem with this attempted solution was that he could never know what that was.

He felt unappreciated and misunderstood. So he arrived at an uneasy unconscious compromise: to maintain his sense of control over fears of humiliation he divorced himself from his work, so that he could be convinced it had nothing to do with him. In essence, he disappeared, leaving something behind that was not himself: his paintings. And he believed that even if he could not be understood or appreciated, his paintings could be. Adam fantasized being "discovered" and becoming famous only after his death.

As the word implies, an *exhibition* means exhibiting and exhibitionism, something Adam craved. Unconsciously he felt continually unseen and overlooked, and ashamed that others might see how much he looked to them for a sense of his own identity. So he invented ever more convincing fantasies of being invisible. But while they solved one set of problems, invisibility fantasies only intensified his anxieties about being totally unrecognizable.

The invisible person has both advantages and disadvantages

over the rest of us, Adam explained to me. The invisible man can take his enemy by surprise, as the film *Diary of an Invisible Man* shows.[3] But then he can also be bowled over by persons who do not see him. Although he has the advantage of surprise in direct confrontation, in ordinary life he is at the mercy of those who knock him about inadvertently because they do not know he is there.

Unfortunately, Adam's invisibility fantasies kept going awry. He began to realize in his analysis that when he withdrew into fantasies of invisibility he became more frightened of being overlooked. As Adam commented, the closer he comes to revealing himself, the more intense the anxiety of being misunderstood as the person he feels himself to be.

In part, then, Adam's fantasies of invisibility intensified fears of being misunderstood. Not wanting me to misunderstand him, he withdrew: his feelings were always outside the frame of the relationship. As he struggled to reveal more of himself to me, he grew more frightened of having me see the way he felt. Unconsciously he realized he was actually the one causing (my) misperceptions of him, as spies mislead enemy governments.

SPY GLASS HILL AND THE RAGE OF PERSONALITY:
ADAM, GRAHAM GREENE, AND KIM PHILBY

For a time then, Adam's obsession with invisibility took the form of a lively interest in spies who look but are not seen to be looking, invisible themselves but defined by their abilities to see. In this context, Adam spoke frequently of both Kim Philby and of Graham Greene, whose psychodynamics were similar to his.

Philby began his career in the British Secret Service by playing "double-cross" disinformation games against the Nazis, prompted in part by his father's rivalry with Lawrence of Arabia, in which his father was pale and paltry when compared with the larger-than-life Lawrence. Philby's father named him Kim, after the Kipling character involved in intrigue and espionage. Philby seems to have been part of a double double-cross operation: while deceiving the crown, and while working for the KGB, Philby might well have been deceiving the Soviets by posing as their agent. Throughout World War II Philby was talking personally to Hitler and Stalin, both of whom considered him particularly reliable. Yet at the same time he was influencing Churchill, who confided in him as well. As Ron Rosenbaum wrote recently of Philby, "All his friendships, his relationships, his marriages become elaborate lies requiring unceasing vigilance to maintain, lies in a play-within-a-play only he can follow. He is not merely the supreme spy; he is above all the supreme actor."[4]

Wondering what made Philby tick, one author speculates that it was a fascination with how closely he could make the various players in the international spy games respond to his information or disinformation. Philby used their responses to feed his imagination. In his unpublished memoirs Philby tells of his childhood attraction for fantasy landscapes and maps. He would draw "a long series of imaginary countries with complicated promontories and inlets and improbably situated hills. My grandmother criticized me for calling all of them 'Spy Glass Hill.'" These maps allowed Philby to believe that he was the creator of the landscape, to imagine a context for himself, to situate or locate himself in fantasy since he could not do so in the real world.

Adam was fascinated with the ambiguity of Philby's power; it was impossible to know whether he was terrorized by the Soviets and forced to remain in Moscow, a helpless failure; whether he repaired to Moscow in order not to suffer humiliation in England; or whether he was able to retain his extraordinary position as the master spy on whose words the most powerful men in the world would hang, a man who could at will confuse both the most clear-sighted and the most devious of his rivals.

Adam himself had been confronted by the following paradox: power is all the more powerful if it is kept hidden, secret, not recognized or "seen," untapped and untouched. Although he had great ambitions and a violent temper, he was inconspicuous in dress and unemphatic and unaggressive in manner. He hid his power like the CIA director William Colby described outwardly as the perfect covert operator: the traditional gray man, so inconspicuous that he would never catch a waiter's eye in a restaurant.[5] And the analysis revealed that Adam's powerful fantasies of secrecy and fascination with Philby served additional functions: they helped to control his feelings of betrayal (by his parents, girlfriends, and business associates) by focusing him obsessively on more effective techniques and means of subterfuge.

Graham Greene, author of *The Third Man*, prided himself on being able to understand the endlessly elusive and enigmatic Philby.

Greene is known for his stout defense of Philby in England, a stance that quite possibly cost Greene his knighthood and even a Nobel Prize. But there were, perhaps, even more masks than Greene originally believed. While Greene assumed Philby was a double agent, working for the KGB, he may actually have been a triple agent, working for the British, an idea that Greene was investigating feverishly before his death.

Like Adam, Greene too suffered an extremely traumatic childhood. He described his headmaster father as "sinister" and "sadistic," and remembered the occasional visitations of his mother to the nursery as "state visits." Subjected to extreme deprivation, an aloof, distant mother, and an inflexible father who could be dealt with only through subterfuge, Greene early on developed an elaborate fantasy life, disguising what was serious, treating trivia as important, and reaching behind the disguise for some semblance of reality. "He wrote serious novels disguised as thrillers, created religious tales filled with doubt, a love story filled with hate, an autobiography which barely mentions his wife and children, a travel book in which the mental journey is more important than the physical one, and a play in which one of the two major characters says only 'yes' and 'no.'"[6]

Moreover, the title of his first novel, *The Man Within* was taken from the Sir Thomas Browne line in *Religio Medici*. "There is another man within me that's angry with me," a notion that applies both to Adam and to Philby. In fact, Greene wrote *The Human Factor* about Philby, using as his common theme the "rage of personality," a theme borrowed from Henry James. Perhaps the best known of Greene's uses of Philby was *The Third Man,* in which the untrustworthy central character, Harry Lime, is a cross between Greene himself (Lime) and Harold Philby (Harry).[7] Incidents from Greene's unhappy childhood appear disguised but unmistakable in his writings, providing evidence that he seemed to be able to access childhood memories only at one remove (i.e., when fictionalized): "the distant mother, the kind gardener, the escape to the pond and the island, the taste of freedom and fear in the Dark Walk, the shed"[8] and the image of himself, "a boy hanging from a cord above a pile of potato sacks," saved by the gardener.[9]

In this context, consider the plot of his short story "The Bear Fell Free." Farrell, a young man who is very drunk, is dared by someone pretending to be his friend to fly his small plane across the Atlantic. His girlfriend ends up sleeping with the false friend while

Farrell sets forth. Farrell is killed in the plane crash, and the only object salvaged from the wreck is a teddy bear, symbol of an attempt to create an adequate context in fantasy, an effort to have something to hold onto when mothers and parents are not there. D. W. Winnicott speaks of teddy bears as quintessentially transitional objects, experienced by the child to be both me and not-me, both mother and not-mother, as a way of having something motherlike to hold onto in her absence.[10]

OEDIPAL SHAME, SPIES, AND FANTASY

The line between reality and fantasy is never clear, and can never be relied upon to bolster a sense of identity, especially when its fluidity is used as a defense against pain and helplessness. In fun Greene often nosed out something real, as when he speculates that Beatrix Potter must have gone through a terrible crisis in her Puddle-Duck period,[11] which it turns out she really had.

Conversely, Green could take horrifying experiences and remove himself from them, transforming them into trifles, Easter hats on display. Of the London bombings, he wrote, "I loved the blitz. It was wonderful to wake up and know you were still alive and hear glass being swept up in the night. . . . In the blackout you could see the stars, something you can no longer do in any city."[12] Greene's intricate, secret, and serious fantasy life, his ability to make light of what is serious, to hide something serious beneath a seeming prank—all point to a retreat from his own life into a world of the imagination. He said to his wife Vivien, "All that is good in me, all that's anything worth having in me, is in the books. What's left is just what's left over."[13]

Speaking of his own fantasies of invisibility by speaking of Greene and Philby, Adam explained that he resembled the spy who thrives on fear and confusion. Spies, he added, want the superpowers (the United States and Russia) to be so afraid of each other that they have to find out what the other side is doing. Consequently, in the context of mutual fear and mistrust, spies become the most powerful of figures because of their ability to feed the enemy false information, to confuse and distract. Essentially spies induce misconceptions, like giving people wrong directions. Yet the professional virtues of deception bring on anxiety. Adam said of Philby:

He could create confusion on a global scale, which means he had to have been confused himself. If you know where your heart is, you go with it. But if you can fool yourself into believing that sometimes your heart is with Communism and at others it is with England depending on where you happen to be, then you are really lost, you have betrayed everything else for something that has been a fantasy. Then you disregard that you've betrayed something and that the something you've betrayed it for is something you don't want. That confusion gives you the power of betraying everyone. That is chilling. At the end of the day, you're out in the cold.

Here Adam's fears have as their backdrop his confusion over reality and fantasy, which, in turn can be related to confusion over sexual identity, abandonment by his father, fears of being exposed by his father to be unacceptable, of competing against him and besting him, and of being defeated at his hands in the most humiliating fashion. All these come into play as part of what I am referring to as "Oedipal shame." As a spy Adam was in danger of being unknown as an undercover agent, so he could be executed summarily without anyone's taking any notice. Only if as a spy he was a *famous* undercover agent would people spare him. But as a famous undercover agent he ran the risk of getting caught in his own web of lies and deceit, and of losing his heart. Whatever way he turned, Adam was confronted by his fear that he could never be who he was.[11]

RECOGNIZING CHOICE IN THE UNSEEN

For Adam, fantasies of invisibility also expressed an angry refusal to appear as others (i.e., his father) wanted. Threatened with Oedipal shame, Adam sought refuge in confusion over who he was. Therefore he felt all the more sensitive to the danger of giving himself up, of not being himself, by conforming to what others wanted him to be. Such feelings of defiance in the face of the expectations of others are powerfully expressed in Ralph Ellison's *Invisible Man*. The protagonist, who is invisible, bitterly comments:

They wanted a machine? Very well, I'd become a supersensitive confirmer of their misconceptions, and just to hold their confidence I'd be right part of the time. Oh, I'd serve them well and

I'd make invisibility felt if not seen, and they'd learn that it could be as polluting as a decaying body, or a piece of meat in a stew. . . . They were the subtle thinkers—would this be treachery? Did the word apply to an invisible man? Could they recognize choice in that which wasn't seen? . . .[15]

While he can avoid the disapproving gaze of others, the invisible man saddles himself with additional difficulties, since he cannot but confound values such as good and evil, honesty and dishonesty, which depend "upon who happens to be looking through him at the time."[16] And he goes on to say that when he tells the truth he doubts himself and is hated, but when "he tried to give [his] friends the incorrect, absurd answers they wished to hear," he was loved.

In my presence they could talk and agree with themselves, the world was nailed down and they loved it. They received a feeling of security. But here was the rub. . . . In order to justify them I had to take myself by the throat and choke myself until my eyes bulged out and my tongue hung out and wagged like the door of an empty house in a high wind.[17]

Such conflicts—between "justifying them" and expressing oneself—seem to me hallmarks of what I am calling "Oedipal shame." Feeling invisible, not having what it takes to be seen by others, means being without any reliable inner gyroscope, which, of course, leaves one empty, essentially disoriented, and cut off. Seen in this light, the fear of disappearing is secretly justified. Behind it lies the anxiety that there is really nothing there, nothing to disappear at all, nothing behind the mask.

OF OEDIPAL BLINDNESS AND OEDIPAL SHAME: LOSS, DISAPPEARANCE, AND RAGE

Yet another patient, Joseph, whose father was blind and died when he was eight years old, described the feeling of not being able to find himself in his father's eyes. "It was like looking into a tunnel." A few years after the death of his father, and a few days before his bar mitzvah, his mother died. He was acutely embarrassed about letting anyone know that his parents were dead. This embarrassment was exacerbated when he was taken in by friends of his father's who expected him to "fit into" their family. When asked who he was, he said his foster parents were his real parents. But that made Joseph feel as though his real parents had never existed, that he was making them disappear.

Joseph felt he could not tell anyone about who he really was, and continually had to act like a member of the "new" family, even though his adoptive father never called him "son," was unsympathetic, and harsh to him, and other members of the family had difficulties accepting him as a real family member. Since they did not recognize him, he could hide from himself. Acutely calibrated to what he thought others needed and wanted him to be, Joseph became an actor. He went in search of audiences. On his recorded telephone message preceeded by an ominous laugh, one heard his resounding voice saying, "You have reached Master Card."

Joseph obliterated his original parents by not telling others of their existence. If he did not talk about them, others would not "see" them, and if others did not "see" them, his real parents did not exist in their eyes. But then he grew anxious that by not telling others of his real parents, he had killed them again, an untenable position that produced intense guilt, isolation, shame, rage, anxiety, and feelings of imposture. In the process, his real story and the traumatic losses of his parents (his childhood) disappeared. Also, if his original parents were "gone," then he could better protect his "new" parents from what he felt was his own poisonous judgment of their inadequacy, a judgment that he could not afford to see was similar to the one he had formulated of his own parents. Making his parents disappear was a retaliation for parental neglect, at the same time as it was a fantasized effort at protection: his parents were beyond his reach, and so safe from his rage. We are reminded here of the "rage of personality" of which Henry James spoke, and that figured in the work of Graham Greene.

Unable to "see" his parents, to imagine them or know what their fantasies of him were (unable to hold them as stable internal objects), Joseph became convinced as a child that he had to become the person his foster parents wanted him to be. The invisibility of his parents in the eyes of everyone else was a reflection of his own hostile wishes. He wished them to disappear because they abandoned him and he did not want reminders of how much he felt like an abandoned, lost child; if his real parents never existed in the eyes of those around him, he was never abandoned. So he made those who "lost" him vanish. Consequently, he could not mourn them.

The invisibility of his parents in this case protected Joseph from his shame in "looking at" his relation to them as a son, from his anger at their having abandoned him, and from his shame in being alone. For Joseph, being not-seen by his father came to stand for his feeling of having been profoundly annihilated as a child, left only with a husk which he still wanted others to find acceptable. His persona as "Master Card" expresses grandiosity as a defense against feeling overlooked and humiliated. While he never fantasized being invisible, the dynamics and the narcissistic vulnerability are similar to those of Adam. Rather than fantasizing he was invisible himself, he unconsciously did away with his parents in an unsuccessful attempt to master the trauma of their deaths.

THE HUNGER ARTIST

These dynamics of narcissistic vulnerability, grandiosity, fears of exposure, and longing to be seen are to be found powerfully conveyed in one of Franz Kafka's most haunting works, "The Hunger Artist." At a time when hunger artists were readily to be found in circuses and sideshows, the prowess of one hunger artist in particular, the most expert of those practitioners of his profession, brought throngs. Some visitors, mostly butchers, stared endlessly at the emaciated figure in his small barred cage.

The hunger artist could have gone on fasting—it seemed easy—but the public and his impresario demanded some restraint. Despite his fame, the hunger artist grew more and more troubled "all the more troubled because no one would take his real trouble seriously."[18] Then fasting began to fall out of fashion, and the hunger artist had to join a circus, where he fasted in his small cage surrounded by animals. But as public interest in the art of fasting waned, the hunger artist felt his heart grow heavy: "it was not the hunger artist who was cheating, he was working honestly, but the world was cheating him of his reward."[19]

Then one day someone noticed that a perfectly good cage was standing empty. The hunger artist was found beneath a pile of straw. "Forgive me," whispered the hunger artist, adding in his last words, "But you shouldn't admire [my fasting]. I have to fast . . . because I couldn't find the food I like. If I had been able to find it, I should have made no fuss and stuffed myself like you or anyone else." After the death of the hunger artist, his cage was cleaned out and then filled anew by a wild panther whose sleekness, appetite, and leaping about the cage brought flocks of delighted spectators.[70]

The "Hunger Artist" expresses with unforgettable vividness one of the central themes of this book: that behind the desire and addictive need for applause, acclaim, fame, and recognition lies the unconscious fear, which amounts to a conviction, that one has lost all hope of ever finding viable sustenance from the outside. Such unconscious shame-laden fears entrench the belief that nobody on the outside can ever see in, and, consequently, that what nobody can recognize cannot exist. The result is unutterably hopeless isolation. The hunger artist exercised his profession because he did not know what to eat, and passed this off as a feat and spectacle, trying in vain to feed on the admiration of spectators as a substitute for the nourishment he could not obtain. The public admired as restraint what he felt to be mortifying deprivation, emptiness, isolation, and helplessness.

SHAME AND PERFORMANCE ANXIETY:
A SHAMED VIOLINIST PLAYS TO A LION

Fantasies of disappearance and invisibility, stage fright, and performance anxieties all strike root in shame conflicts. Where there are anxieties about being misperceived, there are attempts at invention, fantasy, concealment, and subterfuge. Consequently, performance anxiety and fears of exposure induce efforts to correct misperceptions, which, in turn, can induce greater appearance anxiety.

For instance, consider a subplot of Luigi Pirandello's novel *The Notebooks of Serafino Gubbio, Cinematograph Operator, or Shoot.* The protagonist, a cameraman whom we understand will be filming a lion at a later point in the novel, encounters a drunken violinist who never plays his violin, and carries it always beneath a tattered cloth. When the violinist is encouraged to show his violin, which he takes from beneath the cloth, he holds it up "as a modest cripple might expose his stump."[21] We know immediately that the violin is treated as though its possessor were mortally ashamed of it, as though it were a deformed limb, an unspeakable defect. The narrator of the violinist's story, a certain Simone Pau, proves sensitive to the shame of the violinist, saying, "Put away your instrument: I know it hurts you if I tell the story while you have your violin uncovered."

We learn that the violinist used to play when drunk. The more he drank, the more he would play, to the satisfaction of all those around him. But the more he played, the more he drank, and the more money he spent. So after each of these musical evenings, he would pawn his violin in order to pay for his drinks. And then he would be forced to work in order to get his violin back, and the whole cycle of shame, impotence, and defeat would start all over again. Until, one day, someone suggested that he respond to a classified ad in the newspaper, calling for a violinist to accompany a piano. He went for the audition, only to discover that he was supposed to accompany a player piano. That shattered him, and he was never able to look at his violin again, hiding it under a cloth.

At a later point in the novel the nameless violinist appears again, this time enjoined by all to play for the lion, in front of whose cage a crowd has expectantly gathered. The lion roared and pawed the ground. "Play," Simone shouted at him. "Don't be afraid. Play! She will understand you!" Responding to the reassurance that he might be understood, the violinist overcomes his shame. Listen now to Pirandello.

> Whereupon the violinist, as though freeing himself by a tremendous effort from an obsession, at length raised his head, shook it, flung his shapeless hat on the ground, passed a hand over his long, unkempt locks, took the violin from its old green baize cover and threw the cover down also, on top of his hat.
>
> A catcall or two came from the workmen who had crowded in behind us, followed by laughter and comments while he tuned his violin; but a great silence fell as soon as he began to play, at first a little uncertainly, hesitating, as though he felt hurt by the sound of his instrument which he had not heard for so long; then, all of a sudden, overcoming his uncertainty, and perhaps his painful tremors, he managed a few vigorous strokes. These strokes were followed by a sort of groan of anguish, that grew steadily louder, more insistent, strange notes harsh and toneless, a tight coil, from which, every now and then a single note emerged to prolong itself, like a person trying to breathe a sigh amid sobs. Finally this note spread, developed, let itself go, freed from its suffocation, in a phrase melodious, limpid, honey-sweet, intense, throbbing with infinite pain: and then a profound

emotion swept over us all, which in Simone Pau took the form of tears. Raising his arms he signaled to us to keep quiet, not to betray our admiration in any way, so that in the silence this queer, marvelous wastrel might listen to the voice of his soul.

It did not last long. He let his hands fall, as though exhausted, with the violin and bow, and turned to us with a face transfigured, bathed in tears, saying, "There. . . ."[22]

What happened here to free the violinist of his inhibitions? He takes heart when he can feel that his playing can have an effect. And there is also the striking addition of the lion. The violinist is not simply playing to an audience: he is playing to a dangerous beast. Which means that the drunken cycle of shameful impotence symbolized by pawning his violin and working to get it back, a kind of ill-fated Oedipal defeat in which he is constantly humiliated and made to feel useless and contemptible, can be countered: he is not the drunken, ineffective violinist, but rather the master of music so powerful that it can tame lions and stir an audience to tears.

These dynamics are, I think, an inevitable part of all artistic achievement, and perhaps also, of all successful intimate communication. Curiously, it seems to me, writers on performance anxiety have not adequately appreciated the role in artistic motivation of humiliation and fear of isolation, of shame that one's omnipotent fantasies will be exposed and shown to be woefully inadequate and empty, the fear of utter helplessness and humiliation. Perhaps we think we know the danger of exposure to be real, so that the humiliation becomes a "natural" consequence, like trees uprooted after a hurricane. Artists want fame, we think to ourselves, and they therefore expose themselves. But matters are not so simple. When Auden was asked by Stephen Spender whether he (Spender) was any good as a poet, Auden replied frigidly, "Of course. Because you are so infinitely capable of being humiliated. Art is born of humiliation."[23]

These dynamics of humiliation and appearance contribute to not only anxiety but also to physical pain in performers. I have seen a number of artists and musicians for whom physical symptoms appeared as careers were taking off.[24] One patient of mine, a pianist, came to me complaining in the very first session of a debilitating wrist pain that had forced him to abandon the piano as a performer. Preliminary analytic exploration revealed virulent Oedipal struggles with a father who made him practice, but who was absent from the household beginning in early adolescence. The patient developed deep-seated fears of Oedipal defeat and humiliation together with all of the poisoned gifts of Oedipal victory: as an early adolescent he was alone with his mother. Then, in his late teens, just as he was about to attain considerable success, far outstripping his father, his wrist began to hurt and he felt obliged to give up the piano. Simultaneously, these dynamics of Oedipal defeat and humiliation played themselves out with women: with one girlfriend after another he ended up being the "nice guy" with the result that the relationship was not sexual. He lived with many women toward whom he felt strong physical attraction without ever feeling it was legitimate to touch them. In fact, he continually reassured them he would not, and that they were safe with him. The result was frustration, rage, and debilitating humiliation.[25]

SHAME AND CREATIVITY

Discrepancies between the way one imagines one is and the way one feels or imagines one is being seen, between the way one wants to be and the way one fears one is, produce both conscious and unconscious efforts to control the way one appears. The performer cultivates such control, and the musical performer relies upon his technical and physical mastery of his instrument. However, when the body rebels, or when the musical result is experienced as defective, the performer is often at the mercy of fears, verging often on panic, of disappearing.[26]

Whether actors, writers, musicians, or artists, in creative work the individual is never certain of finding his or her way back from the world of fantasy, and in that fact lies terrible fear, shame, and humiliation over being shut out, isolated and ostracized. Seen in this light, what is surprising is not that some performers and artists are stricken by performance anxiety, but that any are not. Those dancers or actors who appear on stage naked, for example, develop what I have come to think of as an imaginary inner proscenium arch that in fantasy frames their ideas about how they are seen and that protects them from the experience of exposure and annihilation. When they use their technical mastery in the service of omnipotent, exhibitionistic wishes, they are that much more vulnerable to performance anxiety, their defenses that much more fragile. When, by contrast, they retain some grip on the line between fantasy and reality, while letting themselves go, when they can use their imaginations and beings to guide technique, they can harness what their performance is about and creatively fantasize the ways they are seen.

In this chapter I have been concerned with fantasies of invisibility and fears of exposure and performance anxiety, suggesting that their dynamics are essentially similar. Not so long ago, the Czech playwright-politician Vaclav Havel gave a short talk on Kafka in accepting an honorary degree from the Hebrew University of Jerusalem.[27] It begins, "This is far from the first honorary degree I have received, but I accept it with the same sensation I always do: deep shame." Going on to say that he feels all his accomplishments have been attempts to "vindicate my permanently questionable right to exist," Havel concludes, "I thank you for the honour, and after what I've said here, I'm ashamed to repeat that I accept it with a sense of shame."

5 I Can't See; I'm Invisible

> How small, of all that human hearts endure,
> That part which laws or kings can cause or cure.
>
> —Samuel Johnson

It is a truism that fears of being found out can lead to lying. In this chapter I will be exploring the extent to which shame, and particularly Oedipal shame, can motivate lying. Often my patients will say that they have avoided or lied out of a fear of exposure. But exposure of what? What can we know about the phenomena and experience of exposure? What makes it painful? In the last chapter, I spoke of fantasies of visibility and invisibility, spies and patients lost in webs of lies and deceit. Can lying make the feeling of isolation and disorientation more palpable? One patient who used to walk alone in a European city was excruciatingly ashamed when he met someone he knew because then his loneliness and isolation would be visible to someone else. Yet hiding it or lying about it, although intended to alleviate his shame, only worsened his sense of isolation.

The story of Secret tells of deceit, shame, and rivalry between mother and daughter. Secret was a hamster who came into a household in which family members often communicated through other members, rather than speaking for themselves. As a very little girl of about six, Emily wanted a hamster. Her mother refused to get her one. So, defiantly and fully aware that her mother would not approve, she went to the store with her pocket money and bought a furry little ball whom she named "Secret." Every day when Emily returned home from school, she would have a couple of hours to take Secret out of the closet in which he lived and play with him before her mother returned. One day the family decided to go on an outing. Emily furtively popped Secret into her leather purse, and the family set forth. But along the way, the hamster gnawed a hole in the purse. As Secret hit the pavement, Emily cried out, "Mummy, Mummy, catch Secret!"

And so Secret was captured with the help of Olympian beings. Calm returned to the house, until Emily decided that Secret was lonely. She set forth to find him an appropriate mate, returning home with a second hamster. All went well until Secret bit her head off, at which point Emily refused to show him any more affection, and never again touched him, picked him up, or kissed him. But her guilt was more than Emily could bear, so she got her brother to kiss Secret on the nose each night.

Emily felt Secret had done an unspeakably damnable thing by biting off the head of his mate. But she at once concealed from herself her anger over Secret's offense, and protected herself from guilt at neglecting the one who depended on her. By getting her brother to do what she could not, she could hide from herself her failure to live up to her expectations (that she would never abandon an animal who depended on her). She protected her ideal of herself by manipulating her brother to fill in for her, thereby saving herself from shame, but at the price of a distortion of reality (hers). Also, such reliance upon other family members to maintain her image and ideal of herself blurred boundaries between herself and other family members, and hid her own shame at not being able to communicate as and for herself.

Let me review the story of Secret in the light of Oedipal shame and the ego ideal. Secret came into the family against the wishes of Emily's mother. From the outset Secret was a symbol of Emily's defiance. Emily strove through the hamster to provide for herself a conflict-free area in which her ideal of herself as capable of affection and bounty could thrive. Not only was hiding Secret covering over an Oedipal shame conflict in which Emily feared she would inevitably lose, but Secret's cannibalistic indulgences led Emily to react with the biting disapproval characteristic of the Queen in *Alice in Wonderland* whose "Off with her head" comes readily to mind.

The subject of an inability to speak for and as oneself brings me back to Pirandello. In his novel *As You Desire Me (Come tu mi vuoi)*

Pirandello uses a character he does not name, "the Strange Lady." The Strange Lady (whom Salter, her former lover, knows as Cia) defies Salter to imagine he can "see" who she is.

> I no longer know I am alive—a body without a name, waiting for someone to take it! Ah well, if he can recreate me, if he can give a soul to this body, which is that of his Cia, let him take it, let him take it, and let him build out of his memories—his own—a beautiful new life—Oh, I am in despair.[1]

Aunt Lena and Uncle Salesio bring out a portrait of Cia, but then set to arguing about whether the portrait bears any resemblance to the Strange Lady. Lena says that the Strange Lady's eyes are green; Uncle Salesio says they are blue. In typically Pirandellian fashion (and reminiscent of "Right You Are If You Think You Are"), the Strange Lady comments sadly that what is green for Lena is blue for Salesio.[2] And she adds, pointedly, "We do not all see with the same eyes!"[3] Then she says,

> Look at me—here in the eyes—not them! These eyes have no longer seen for me; they have no longer been my own eyes, not even for looking at myself. They have been like this—like this— in yours—always—because there has been born in them, out of those eyes of yours, my own aspect, as you saw me! the aspect of all things, of all life, as you saw it!

And she says bitterly and reproachfully, remarking upon the contemptible attempts on the part of others to recognize her, to reconstruct her, stone upon stone, like the villa,

> You've made a poor search for your Cia! You lost no time in rebuilding the villa for her; but you have not looked, you have not thought of looking, to see if, among the scattered stones, the rubbish and the ruins, there might have been left something of hers, something of her soul . . . some memory that is really live— for her! not for you![4]

WHEN I DON'T SEE YOU I CAN INVENT YOU BETTER: THE ANALYSIS OF SUSAN

In my work as an analyst, I have been impressed again and again by how valiantly my patients struggle to reclaim something essential of themselves through the analytic process, and by how important it is to realize what each needs to reclaim from me and through me. I come to know these struggles through understanding how my patients see me, how they imagine me, and how they imagine I see (and imagine) them. In many patients the struggle to become recognizable, if not analyzed with an eye to shame dynamics, can be damaging, like a heart beating out of control.

One day several years into the analysis, as Susan came in the door I noticed that she was not looking at me. Overcoming my own shame at having taken so long to notice something so fundamental, I pointed out to her that she never looked at me. Knowing her to be witheringly critical, I braced myself for what would follow. But, contrary to my expectations, there was no outburst, indeed no visible emotion at all. She responded by saying offhandedly and as though it were the most obvious thing in the world that she avoided my gaze so as to "invent me better." So long as I was not real, she did not have to contend with imagining that she was different in my eyes than she was in her own.[5] When I wondered aloud why she did not look at me, she replied, "If I really looked at you, I might find that you are really 'potato eaters,' like the Van Gogh painting. . . . That you are too real. . . . That for you things are what they are. I have trouble accepting that."

Susan found it difficult to imagine herself through my eyes and tried to disregard whatever she found inconvenient or uncomfortable in what I saw of her. If she changed the color of her nail polish, she would begin the session saying in admonishing tones, "Don't say anything at all about my nail polish." Commenting on her attempts to audition for a part in a play, she mused,

> I was not acting when I did the reading. If I play a role which draws on parts of me you have not seen (and which other people have not seen either), then if I play the role badly, that means that maybe I am not what I think I am . . . I'm stuck, nobody wants me. I'm caught between two worlds, and I don't really want to find out that nobody wants me.

Like the Strange Lady, Cia, Susan keeps feelings of unrecognizability and abandonment at bay by playing her part well, judging herself by the reactions of others. (Do *they* think she is playing "well?") As subsequent analytic work showed, Susan feared that she would be unable to make herself over in my eyes. As I realized how uneasy I felt, I began to be aware of the rage, shame, fear, and hope symbolized by her averted gaze. Rene Spitz (1957) noted that the infant can demonstrate choice by head movements, that is, by what she looks at (or does not look at). Caparrota (1989) has suggested that if the mother finds it difficult to cope with the infant's gaze (even at fourteen months), the gaze-avoidance on the part of the infant can be seen as a defense against the annihilation anxiety triggered by the infant's looking to the mother for a response that is not there. For the infant, there is no locating the nonresponse in the mother, since it is felt as the most primitive annihilation anxiety.

DO YOU WANT ME TO BE SOMEONE ELSE?

Because she was so uncertain of who she was in my eyes (how well she played "the part"), Susan repeatedly expressed a wish to disappear, to hide beneath a stone. While such a wish might seem to solve the problem of having others get her wrong, it also exacerbated her deep, unalterable isolation and fears of abandonment. At times she wondered whether if she starved herself and lost too much weight, her parents would ever take notice. Would she have to disappear before they noticed anything was wrong? Susan dreamed of being unhitched and of vanishing, an indication of how fragile she felt the connection between us to be.

> My mechanic is driving me to my car in his car, a black and very large, Oldsmobile cutlass, a '76 perhaps. I see my car being towed away. My sister wanted me to exchange it for another. She said she was getting a "daisy-cavalry." The car she saw was blue, but was soft on the outside. Then she saw her "new" car. It was yellow. Hitched to the back there was a little cart, with a little black girl sitting in it. Somehow she became unhitched, turned into the left hand turn lane, and vanished.

Several themes in this dream bear noting: that of a car (her ability to enter into relationships and get about in the world), that of seeing her car being towed away (her helplessness), and, finally, that of a little girl sitting alone in an unhitched cart disappearing into the left-hand turn lane.

As her analysis progressed, Susan's awareness of her inability to give voice to her feelings intensified fears of disappearing. Repeatedly she dreamed that the volume was turned down on her voice. Gradually, through talking about her teddy bears, quintessentially transitional objects two of which slept with her, she began to express herself more insistently.

> My teddy bear never talked when I was a child. It is beginning to talk now. I can talk for it. I never used to understand kids who had imaginary friends or things like that. I think I was a very unimaginative child. I was always being told that I should grow up. When I was seventeen, I felt as though I was forty. I always thought my mother really wanted me to be someone else, but never told me. I used to ask her if she did not want to trade me in. Do you want me to be someone else? My boyfriend does. . . . I used to wish all the time that someone would know how sad I was when I was a child and come to my room and speak to me. Nobody did. Then I would get difficult, and my mother would come just so I would not scream so much. Then I would feel guilty that she had to come.

Feeling that I (or her boyfriend) want her to be someone else is an important transference theme: in her dream her car was towed away and traded in. But here she is able to begin to give voice to the pain of her isolation, sadness, abandonment, and shame ("I used to wish that someone would know how sad I was").

PEEKABOO, DISAPPEARANCE, AND THE GAME OF THE BOBBIN

Once I began to understand that there was an entire world in the meanings of Susan's not looking at me, I became more aware of her struggles with disappearance/abandonment/isolation. Speaking of her fears about weekend separations, I commented that children try to master fears of maternal abandonment by playing peekaboo. To my astonishment, Susan responded categorically that she never played like that at all. When she played peekaboo, she did so not to make a toy or her mother appear; *she did so to make herself disappear.*

At this point let me review briefly Freud's discussion of the dynamics of peekaboo. This appears in a famous passage in *Beyond the Pleasure Principle* dealing with the playing habits of an eighteen-month-old boy whom Freud had occasion to observe. This little fellow had the distressing habit "of taking any small objects he could get hold of and throwing them away from him into a corner, under the bed, and so on, so that hunting for his toys and picking them up was often quite a business."[6] As the child threw the objects he "gave vent to a loud, long-drawn out 'o-o-o-', accompanied by an expression of interest and satisfaction."

Yet, Freud noted,

> the only use he made of any of his toys was to play "gone" with them. . . . The child had a wooden reel with a piece of string tied round it. It never occurred to him to pull it along the floor behind him, for instance, and play at its being a carriage. What he did was to hold the reel by the string and very skillfully throw it over the edge of the curtained cot, so that it disappeared into it, and the same time uttering his expressive "o-o-o-o-o." He then pulled the reel out of the cot again by the string and hailed its reappearance with a joyful "da" [there]. This, then, was the complete game—disappearance and return. As a rule one only witnessed its first act, which was repeated untiringly as a game in itself, though there is no doubt that the greater pleasure was attached to the second act.[7]

Freud focuses on the child's attempt to master through play the fear of the loss of the object which, in *Inhibitions, Symptoms, and Anxiety,* he maintains is the prototype of anxiety. In his view, the game entails the child's "great cultural achievement," the renunciation of instinctual satisfaction that he "had made in allowing his mother to go away without protesting." For Freud, the game turns a passive situation—in which the child was helpless to prevent his mother from leaving—into an active one;[8] the pleasure in throwing away the objects expresses the child's anger at his mother for going away. The gesture has "a defiant meaning: 'All right, then, go away! I don't need you. I'm sending you away myself.' "Children play at losing and finding bobbins in order to master the trauma of the loss of the object (the mother). By controlling the bobbin, Freud suggests, they fantasize controlling the mother, and by controlling the mother, controlling their own rage.[9]

But whereas Freud emphasizes the child's attempt to master through play the fear of the loss of the object, for Susan the situation is radically different; she plays to make *herself* disappear. One might then think that there are two rather opposite ways in which the game of the bobbin can be played. The first (the one on which Freud focuses) is about mastery and separateness, and the tolerance of loss. The second (the one on which Susan focuses), is about crushing defeat, coming up against impossible odds (Oedipal shame), and disappearing.[10]

I AM INVISIBLE; I CAN'T SEE MYSELF

It is a strange paradox that when one cannot imagine how one is seen, one must remain invisible. Some months after the interactions just described, Susan contracted an ulcer on her retina, as a result of which she had to stop wearing her contact lenses and resort to glasses. Glasses, she thought, made her look blind; her "coke bottle" lenses were so thick they called everyone's attention to her poor vision. Too ashamed to come to see me for a week, she began her first session back sobbing, "I am invisible. I can't see myself. I can't look at myself in the mirror. Unless I get a few inches from my nose, I can't see anything at all. I don't know who I am."[11] Habitually reserved and restrained, Susan in these sessions opened the floodgates.

> It's all I have, my looks. But I can't do anything about making myself look OK. I am just going to look sorry, since I can only look like someone ordinary trying to look like more than they are capable of. . . . My looks are all I had and I don't have them anymore. Other people don't notice me because I am forgettable. . . . I can't stand to go out and be invisible. People look through me because I'm nobody, I'm nothing. . . . There is nothing I can do. I can't even see myself.
>
> If I could do something and look at someone when I'm talking, if I could go outside and feel someone could see me, then I could do things. Now I know people think I'm just another nobody making noise. . . . I can't talk to people and make them notice me. I don't feel like a person. I can't get what I want out of people. They say I look fine. Fine for being a nobody, for being invisible. In my interactions with people I can't express the things I usually do with my face, since it's not there. . . . In the past I could look at that person when I'm talking. And if they didn't pay attention, they had to make an *effort* to ignore me, not because they just could. Now since I look like

a nobody I can't communicate with people as I usually do. What they see is not me. They can't see me the way I want to be seen because I'm not there. . . .

And when I related what she was saying to her feelings about me in the transference, she discounted me dismissively.

Often I don't look at you. I guess if I do look at you, then I have to admit that you can see me. If you can see me, then I'm afraid you can see me hiding. But since you are not nearly as percep- tive as I want you to be, it probably doesn't matter.

All those pieces of everything I put together to make myself feel like an interesting person I don't have now. . . . It's like the invasion of the body snatchers. They come and take your body. They act like they're you, but they're not. I'm really upset, but I don't know it because someone took over my body. It looks like me and sounds like me, but I'm not there.

Like Sam, Susan fantasized about disappearing; like him she suffered from intense Oedipal (which includes pre-Oedipal) shame and rivalry with the same sex parent. And like Sam too, she could not unconsciously imagine there was any place for her in the minds of her parents. In describing Odysseus, Gottfried Keller describes the shame of not belonging, of hiding and being condemned to wander.[12]

If you are wandering about in a foreign land, far from your home and from all that you hold dear, if you have seen and heard many things, have known sorrow and care, and are wretched and for- lorn, then without fail you will dream one night that you are coming near to your home; you will see it gleaming and shining in fairest colors, and the sweetest, dearest, and most beloved forms will move towards you. Then suddenly you will become aware that you are in rags, naked and dusty. You will be seized with a nameless shame and dread, you will seek to find covering and to hide yourself, and you will awake bathed in sweat. This, so long as men breathe, is the dream of the unhappy wanderer.

SEEING, BEING SEEN, AND MATTERS OF PRIVACY

"The invisible woman"[13] was convinced she had no face and fanta- sized that she had a paper bag over her head. Her dynamics are sim-

ilar to those of Susan; both wanted to punish her parents for not seeing her.[14] Both patients harbored a secret wish to be found. Both can
be related to the curse of contemporary anonymity. Recently a young
woman was discovered dead in New York. Nobody knew she was
missing; nobody knew her; nobody came forward to claim her body.
As one writer observed,

> It was not only her death that was haunting, but a kind of root-
> lessness among us that death suggests, the notion that the
> anonymity of this city is only a shade removed from invisibility,
> and that the price of privacy may be to die alone.[15]

All forms of "not-seeing" hide the pain and conflict inherent in
the self-consciousness of being ashamed, which itself must, out of
shame, go overlooked and unseen. In a recent article, Milan Kundera[16] calls attention to appearance anxiety and shame phenomena.

> I am looking at a window across the way. Toward evening the
> light goes on. A man enters the room. Head lowered, he paces
> back and forth; from time to time he runs his hand through his
> hair. Then, suddenly, he realizes that the lights are on and he can
> be seen. Abruptly he pulls the curtain. Yet he wasn't counter-
> feiting money in there; he had nothing to hide but himself, the
> way he walked around the room, the sloppy way he was
> dressed, the way he stroked his hair. His well-being depended on
> his freedom from being seen.

And, in the spirit of this book, he continues,

> Shame is one of the key notions of the Modern Era. . . . One of
> the elementary situations in the passage to adulthood, one of the
> prime conflicts with parents, is the claim to a drawer for letters
> and notebooks, the claim to a drawer with a key; we enter adult-
> hood through the *rebellion of shame* [emphasis added].[17]

To imagine what we are looking at, to imagine ourselves looking and being looked at while looking—all seem essential to our
sense of who we are, and to some basic confidence in the continuity
of our lives. Susan's anxieties about not having a face, and about not
being recognizable because she herself cannot see, provide a poignant
example of how powerful and how toxic are the dynamics of Oedi-

pal shame. Instead of playing at "gone" to master the loss of her mother, she used the game to fantasize about disappearing herself. When out of a fear of what is imagined, we construe our lives in terms of appearances, we needlessly restrict the compass of our lives and thereby place our identities at risk.

6 What the Camera Sees

The Tragedy of Modern Heroes and "The Rules of the Game"

I shall constantly ferret out the musical in the idea, the situation, and so on, distilling its very essence, and then when I have made the reader so musically receptive that he seems to hear the music though he really hears nothing, then I shall have completed my task, then I become mute, then I say to the reader as to myself: listen.

—Soren Kierkegaard

In the work of Luigi Pirandello the tension between the various ways one is seen—and the dependency on others to provide acceptable, recognizable images of oneself—leads to excruciating attempts to hide and control the ways one is perceived. These tensions also underlie Jean Renoir's film *The Rules of the Game*, the title of which may well have been borrowed from the title of the play that Pirandello's *Six Characters* were trying to stage. In Renoir, as in Pirandello, whatever is experienced as fully "inside" can never be expressed; the only way characters can know each other is by the "outside" on which each depends so heavily. All that can be revealed is the stake each character has in controlling the way he or she is seen by others, thereby allowing us to feel (and imagine) something of what is going on inside the outside. This impression is conveyed technically by special lenses that Renoir used to keep depth in focus throughout the film. These were "special lenses, very fast lenses, but ones that gave us considerable depth, so that we could keep our backgrounds in focus almost all the time."[1]

Essentially the film follows the career of the pilot André Jurieu, whose heroic status conflicts impossibly with his love for Christine de la Chesnaye, a German aristocrat married to the French Marquis de la Chesnaye in whose château (La Colinière) the film largely takes place. The prominence and public stature of Jurieu's victory at having traversed the Atlantic Lindbergh-style diverge markedly from the vulnerability of the private man, who feels that he is nobody if he does not have Christine's love. From the time his plane touches the runway and the crowds go wild as the film begins, Jurieu is recklessly prepared to cast aside his newly won fame and international prominence for the love of Christine.

The go-between who allows Jurieu and Christine to meet is the ne'er-do-well, bon vivant Octave (played by Renoir himself). Octave has neither profession nor vast inheritance, and therefore is entirely dependent on Le Chesnaye and his aristocratic friends. At Jurieu's insistence, Octave agrees to persuade Le Chesnaye to invite Jurieu to a weekend gathering of his friends (including his wife Christine) who intend to feast, hunt, and amuse themselves at his château.

The plan goes awry, however, when the unaristocratic Jurieu proves too serious-minded for Le Chesnaye to ignore; Le Chesnaye's usual aristocratic defense of supreme indifference simply does not work on Jurieu, who unrealistically wants Le Chesnaye's permission to pursue Christine. By a curious twist of plot, both Le Chesnaye, the owner of the château, and Schumacher, its zealous, plebeian guardian and gamekeeper, find themselves cuckolded, Le Chesnaye by Octave and Shumacher by Marceau. But while Le Chesnaye attempts to ignore the situation, Schumacher, brandishing and shooting his rifle, chases Marceau and Lisette, his wife, while the guests scurry for cover.

On the surface, then, the film depicts a clash of worlds: that of Jurieu, the self-made man; of Le Chesnaye and his aristocracratic guests; and that of Marceau, Schumacher, and the ordinary folk. As the unforgettable and magnificently corpulent cook says of one particularly capricious guest who has just instructed him not to put salt in her food, "I can deal with proper diets, but not with whims, " all the while pouring in vast quantities of salt. Renoir frames the discrepancy between visions and ideals of the self, on the one hand (stories told by the characters to one another about themselves), and the realities of daily life and social status on the other. At the climax of the film chaos and passions erupt in what has become known as the Walpurgis Night sequence, shattering the illusions of appearance, until the end when all is put back in its box, like a child's toys before bedtime.

The film opens with crowds thronging to greet the public hero, André Jurieu. The camera gets jostled and swept up in the movement of the mass. One female reporter attempts to get a statement out of Jurieu, expecting some commentary about the difficulty of his feat, some expression of hesitation or fear, some "human interest" statement of his experience of flying. But she gets nothing at all, save an expression of dismay because Christine is not there to greet him.

Right from the start there is little or no correspondence between the public fantasies of heroism and the behavior of our hero. Jurieu comes out of the skies a hero, but once on the ground proves egregiously ill-equipped to deal with those around him, disinclined either to recognize or to play by "the rules of the game." Only if he had played his role as hero and instigator of fantasies, might he have been able to stand up and be counted in the world of La Colinière. That, of course, is what he cannot do, unable as he is to recognize himself in the fantasies others have of him. As Octave (Renoir) testily snaps at him, "Instead of modestly conforming to your role as national hero, you blurt out your dismay at not seeing Christine." Later Octave comments that the tragedy of Jurieu is the tragedy of all modern heroes: "he is capable of traversing the Atlantic, but cannot even cross the Champs Elysées outside the pedestrian crossing."[2] Once on the ground, so dull and flat-footed is he that he becomes the most conventional, unromantic, and boring of guests, incapable of the slightest bound of imagination. When at last Jurieu has the chance to run off with Christine, Jurieu insists upon informing Le Chesnaye, her husband.

FREE ASSOCIATION AND OPEN FORM

The Rules of the Game draws upon an approach to detail and relative importance that bears striking similarities to psychoanalytic free association, in which patients say what comes to mind.[3] Poised with "evenly hovering attention," the camera attends equally to small and large details. When Octave first asks Le Chesnaye to invite Jurieu, the scene is shot through a vase of lilies. While this suggests the purity of his motives, the lilies are as important as what he says in conveying the need for an illusion of innocence, which Octave maintains in the eyes of the other characters right up to the end of the film. Renoir's technique of keeping the background in focus also contributes to the sense of freedom with which viewers can take in the various levels of activity in the film. As Renoir's camera registers superimposed activities, so the analyst seeks to attend to everything the patient says (and does not say), absorbed with the twists and turns of free association, and saying to himself, "Now *this* is important," and then "No it's *that.*"

Louis Menand[4] observes that the technical term for the quality that movies like *The Rules of the Game* share is *open form.*

> The camera directs its gaze with equal empathy at every facet of the world viewed. Ordinary things are not scanted or rushed over, since the gods, if there are any, are probably in the details; but grand things are not put into quotation marks either, or set up to be knocked down, since great emotions are as much a part of life as anything else. The door is opened onto the world "as it is," without scrims or stage directions; and the world is left, at the end, in the same condition, unarranged, and unboxed by moral resolution.

The camera deliberately avoids significant cues and simplification; it follows all of the various bits and pieces of the narratives wherever they go, as it follows the screw from the mechanical warbler that Le Chesnaye drops accidentally while walking through the hall.[5] Details are presented like bits and pieces of reality, all equally small and equally insignificant, such that there is no way of telling what is really going to be important later on as the story unfolds. Small things become powerful. Significant comments seem pro forma. The shifting scale of events, both internal and external, lends an imaginary quality to the film, and allows us to feel that we as viewers have the power to make large things small and small things large by thinking them so.

A profoundly sinister theme permeates the film: the rise of Nazism and the denial of the dangers of the world (both internal and external). The film was made in 1939, on the eve of the war when many refused to acknowledge the dangers on the horizon. Most audiences in 1939 received the film with "obvious loathing."[6] In explaining this fact, Renoir commented that nobody likes a portrait of people "dancing on a volcano," adding, "They recognized themselves. People who commit suicide do not care to do so in front of a witness." The dark shadow of war falls on the buffoonery of Octave, on his tainted seductiveness in making plans to run off with Christine, and his seduction of Schumacher's wife.

OF DISGUISES, MECHANISMS, AND MUSIC BOXES

This "open form" approach to camera work, to acting and to directing in terms of "evenly hovering attention," lets viewers lose themselves in the moment, imagining what might be the outcome. As a result of this technique, Renoir follows the stake each character has in maintaining an image of himself or herself. No character is honest, no character altogether what he seems; all have reasons to control what others see of them. For example, after Jurieu's death the young woman who is his age and has obviously had a crush on him from the outset, breaks down in tears. Christine admonishes her, saying that she must compose herself because "people are watching." And the audience is watching too.

As in the world of Pirandello, the fact that it is impossible to avoid those who are watching leads to deceit and masks. And it also leads to the impulse to clown. When Pirandello was informed that he had received the Nobel Prize and was asked by photographers to pose for a considerable time at his typewriter, he typed again and again, filling pages, the word *pagliaccetta* (clown show).

In the stage directions for *Six Characters*, Pirandello instructs the characters to wear masks.

> The characters should not appear like phantasms but like created realities, unchanging constructions of the imagination. . . . The masks will give the impression of faces devised by art and fixed immutably in the fundamental emotional expression suitable to each character, such as remorse for the Father, vengeance for the Daughter, suffering for the Mother (she with fixed wax tears . . .).

And these stage directions echo the importance of masks in Pirandello's plays. Henry in "Henry IV" has trouble composing himself at all; he dyes his hair badly and blotches the rouge on his cheeks. Donna Matilde notes that the portrait of herself as a young woman looks more like her daughter than like herself.

In *The Rules of the Game* the guests, eager to be amused, all don disguises. To the background music of a Mozart march, an infernal machine has been set into motion. While the guests scramble to control the murderously jealous Schumacher, who runs through the château shooting wildly at Marceau, Octave is frantically trying to get someone to take off his bear costume.[7] One haunting symbol of the desperate attempts to conceal and "clown over" what nobody controls is the piano playing by itself. At first the piano is played by the most visible, because the most corpulent, of the female guests. Then, she sits back, disappears from view, and the camera zooms in on the keys playing invisibly.

Surrounded by music boxes, Le Chesnaye serves as the symbol of order, however mechanical and desiccated. In the world of La Colinière he "works," as do his music boxes. When speaking to Marceau about his agonies over the women in his life, Le Chesnaye adopts the same passionless tone of voice used for official occasions. Whatever his desires, whatever his pain, his sense of decorum frames his image of himself in what he imagines to be (and in what appears to be) the eyes of the world. At the opening of the masked theatrical performance, Le Chesnaye's newest and most elaborate music box is unveiled, staged, and revealed as will be the various characters in disguises.

In the final scene, with unexpected irony Le Chesnaye comments apropos of Jurieu, who has just been shot, that "he knew so well how to make us forget he was a hero." At the film's close Le Chesnaye gives a public discourse for the benefit of the guests and the external world, that Schumacher made a justifiable mistake in shooting Jurieu, lights go off, and the film ends. When Le Chesnaye closes the doors to the château and tells everyone to go back to bed, he mechanically puts the lid back on Pandora's box, and provides evidence that the machine still whirls, its figures turn and pirouette.

EVERYONE HAS HIS REASONS

In his novel, *Shoot,* Pirandello describes the constrictions of houses in a manner altogether suitable for the château of Le Chesnaye, in which furniture and people seem to be stage decorations.

I can never understand how certain pieces of furniture can fail to cause if not actually distress at least annoyance, furniture which we dare not venture upon with any confidence, because it seems to have been placed there to warn us with its rigid, elegant grace, that our anger, our grief, our joy must not break bounds, nor rage and struggle, nor exult, but must be controlled by the rules of good breeding. Houses made for the rest of the world, with a view to the part that we intend to play in society; houses of outward appearances, where even the furniture around us can make us blush if we happen for a moment to find ourselves behaving in some fashion that is not in keeping with that appearance nor consistent with the part that we have to play.[8]

Le Chesnaye must, at all costs, play his role; he must abide by the rules of the game, however unhappy he might be. All he can show to the world is the mechanical host, so like the mechanical birds of which he is so proud.

Essentially, Renoir's characters respond to what others see them to be, but can never be whole, can never be intelligible to one another. In no way are they conscious selves which, Rousseau-like, can agree or not agree to enter into contracts with society, for their psychic reality consists in being aware of how they are seen for responding as they do to the appearances, masks, and deceits of others. Which lends weight to Octave's comment that the most horrifying thing about human beings is that everyone "has his reasons." There are the private and infernally secret reasons upon which the intelligibility of outward manifestations depends. These are necessarily hidden, unrepresentable, alluded to but forever out of reach. When at the opening of the film Marceau explains to Le Chesnaye (and to Schumacher) that he poaches to help out his aged mother, Schumacher dismisses such "reasons" as preposterous fabrications. When Geneviève, Le Chesnaye's former lover, wants Le Chesnaye to kiss her, she gives as her reason that she wants to close her eyes and believe things are as they were three years previously, before his marriage to Christine. Geneviève wants to stage a time lost, to imagine something that is not or is no longer, and asks for help in so doing.

Far deeper than the use of Jurieu to point up the vagaries of the French aristocracy, a theme about which oceans of ink have been spilled, lies the ominous theme, "now we must play our parts." As Pirandello's characters must play themselves (and cannot be played by actors), Renoir's characters too must "play themselves." In both, this fact lends a frenetic air to the truncated narratives that the characters attempt to live out, as though each were lunging for what, in the other, might if appropriated lessen their pain and despair. When Christine goes out with St. Aubin, obviously to go to bed with him, she says, "I've had enough of this play." Yet play is all they are capable of, as the alternative is being hopelessly imprisoned, nailed to "the fixedness of life," as Pirandello called it.[9] As Leone Gala says in Pirandello's *Rules of the Game,* the play performed by the Six Characters, "When a fact happens, it stands there, like a prison, shutting you in." The primary defense against such facts in the world both of Pirandello and of Renoir is to imagine, and then not to let on to anyone (and often not to oneself) the extent to which one has done so. The result is isolation and protective deceit.

Jurieu can serve as an escape from the "fixedness of life" only as long as others can believe he is a hero. But Jurieu cannot and will not play the hero, any more than the Father in *Six Characters* can allow himself to imagine that he will be played by an actor.[10] The Father explains that what for the actors is "an illusion that has got to be created for us is our only reality. . . ." But for both Renoir and Pirandello there is despair over the possibility of ever getting what is essential or real across at all.

DECEIT, DENIAL, HONOR, AND THE RULES OF THE GAME

In the two themes of the hunt and the masked ball, frivolity and death run a collision course. Those who fail to play by the rules are either killed like game (Jurieu), or pushed out (Octave, Schumacher, and Marceau). The scrambling of the rabbits, grouse, and pheasant in the hunt scene is echoed by the scrambling of the guests in the masked ball scene in which Schumacher runs wild in his pursuit of Marceau. Chaos is unleashed when rules are not abided by. Beneath the empty rules of the game lie the impending doom and disaster of the war that no amount of denial or attempted control can ward off.

Jurieu fails to play his role as national hero; Schumacher fails to play his role as faithful servant, letting his jealousy for his wife Lisette overrun his sense of duty; Marceau fails to play his role as the sly poacher-turned-domestic by overstepping his part and seducing Schumacher's wife; and Octave, who has seduced virtually all the women in the château, oversteps his bounds by forcing Jurieu on Le

Chesnaye in the first place. Because Jurieu, Octave, and Marceau put their own feelings before respect for context, they threaten the very foundation of the social order.

But the social order is not simply the usual notion of class. Renoir situates social order in the superegos of his characters; it is the ideals to which they aspire and of which they fall short, and the ways in which these ideals fuel denial, together with the shame thereby engendered, which drive their infernal machine. A Winnicottean might object, pointing out that the fundamental problem is inauthenticity. But psychologically, the meaning of "authentic" and "fake" cannot exclude the way in which internal experiences of authenticity or fakeness are known by others. Playing a role, as does Le Chesnaye or Octave, does not necessarily mean that the role is imposed and beneath it there is an authentic self unhappy and in pain struggling heroically to be released from bondage (e.g., Octave struggling to get out of his bear costume). For the film is not really about heroism or the desirability of being strong or honest, authentic or forthright. Within the world of La Colinière there is no possibility of heroism, except perhaps in the service of denial and self-deceit. Perhaps Renoir felt in 1939 that heroism was dead: there was only deceit and more self-deceit, masks and more masks. On his eightieth birthday Renoir wrote,

> Old age is hypocritical and jogs along without knowledge of its victims. I examine myself carefully in the mirror. My face hasn't changed. The features are the same, but that doesn't say very much: have I not repeated a hundred times that human beings wear masks? What I have before my eyes is nothing but an appearance. Behind this appearance, I sense another person, a secret and mysterious person who often acts in defiance of my will, another me who is only waiting for the opportunity to absorb me. I feel panic-stricken.[11]

In many respects the world of Renoir calls up that of Nicholas Gogol whose narratives combine irony, comedy, and tragedy in unforgettable combinations, and whose lively attention to inanimate details contrasts markedly with the dullness and emptiness of his characters. It is this detail that comes to life; the characters function as carriers of detail, little more, as their own sad lives shrink into obscurity. In "The Overcoat," it is the overcoat, not its owner, which takes center stage. In "The Nose," it is the nose itself that assumes a life of its own, mocking the vain, status conscious vacuity of its owner, Kovalev, who sees it around town, addresses it as such, and finds himself outraged at the inconvenience caused by its disobedience. When the clerk to whom Kovalev turns to find his nose offers the unfortunate Kovalev some snuff, Kovalev retorts, "I do not understand how you find it possible to joke. Can you not see that I precisely lack what's needed for a pinch of snuff?"[12] And when a police officer finds the nose, he (the police officer) is described in a deliberately anonymous manner ("of handsome appearance, with quite plump cheeks and side-wiskers neither light nor dark"). When asked how he had found the nose, the policeman replied, "The strange thing was that I myself first took him for a gentleman. But fortunately I was wearing my spectacles, and I saw at once that he was a nose."[13]

Describing appearances and what lies beneath them, Herman Melville writes in his novel *Pierre, or the Ambiguities,*

> Ten million things were as yet uncovered to Pierre. The old mummy lies buried in cloth on cloth; it takes time to unwrap this Egyptian king. Yet now, forsooth, because Pierre began to see through the first superficiality of the world, he fondly weens he has come to the unlayered subtance. But, as far as any geologist has yet gone into the world, it is found to consist of nothing but surface stratified on surface to its axis, the world being nothing but superinduced superficies. By vast pains we mine into the pyramid; by horrible gropings we come to the central room: with joy we espy the sarcophagus; but we lift the lid—and no body is there!—appallingly vacant and vast is the soul of a man![14]

7 Satan, Shame, and the Fragility of the Self

> The biggest danger, that of losing oneself, can pass off in the world as quietly as if it were nothing: every other loss, an arm, a leg, five dollars, a wife, etc. is bound to be noticed.
>
> —Soren Kierkegaard, *Sickness Unto Death*

This chapter focuses on the shame of feeling excluded (being outside) beginning with Adam and Eve, and relating the intolerable shame of isolation to Aristotle's definition of man as a social animal, to the Christian tradition, and to the "sickness unto death" of which Kierkegaard, the early nineteenth-century Danish philosopher (d. 1855), speaks. Profane means literally "outside the fane" (ME, "sacred place"). And the term *holy* stems from words designating wholeness, well-being, and completeness. What is unholy is then, by extension, the fragmentary, the incomplete, and the defective.

Our word *religion* is generally thought to come from the Latin *religio* meaning "that which binds." The words *ligature, ligate,* and *legatto,* the Italian terms used to designate connection in musical notation, all come from the same Latin root, *ligare,* meaning to "bind together." For Aristotle and the ancient Greeks, *anagnorisis,* "the movement from ignorance to the acknowledgement of the other"[1] girds notions of tragedy. In the Christian tradition most writers assumed that the term designated man's bond with God. For the sociological tradition of Saint-Simon, Auguste Comte, Emile Durkheim, Robertson-Smith, and others, religion is defined not by doctrine but rather by its binding effect; it is a social force that brings people together, a notion that serves as the keystone of his monumental *Les Formes éleméntaires de la vie religiuese* (Elementary forms of religious life) (1912) in which he distinguishes between the realms of the sacred (the religious and the social) and the profane (what is not religious). In this book, society is God and God is society hypostatized. Durkheim argues for a religious sociology, focusing attention on what binds (*la solidarité sociale*),[2] an emphasis that has been picked up by such contemporary sociologists as Thomas Scheff and René Girard, who approach notions of the social bond through fears of ostracism and anxieties over exclusion.

The story of Adam and Eve in *Genesis*[3] draws upon fears of being pushed out, of being "outside the fane." John Milton's treatment in *Paradise Lost,* links looking, abandonment anxiety, shame, inside and outside.[4] As the story opens Satan, having been thrown out of Heaven, lurks enviously outside the walls of the Garden of Eden; at the end of the story, God drives Adam and Eve from the Garden. The story makes clear one major difference between God and mankind. God does not have to worry about the limitations of inside/outside, since He is everywhere at the same time. By contrast, Satan and mortals are limited; if they are in, they are not out, and if out, they are not in. Therein lie the seeds of separation anxiety and fears of abandonment.

SIN'S OUT AND OUT'S SIN

The Renaissance painter Massacio represents Adam and Eve covering their eyes as an angel drives them in disgrace from Eden.[5] Adam and Eve could be lowering their eyes so as not to see God looking disapprovingly at them, like the Lilliputians who cannot stand to have Gulliver see them. By not looking, Adam and Eve deny their loss: the loss of the social bond and separation and/or abandonment by God. Paul Ricoeur[6] suggests that sin is "the loss of a bond, of a root, of an ontological ground." Like Oedipus who as an infant was abandoned and left to die, Adam and Eve are abandoned, left unprotected outside the walls, in a quintessentially asocial, shameful, profane state, "utterly and absolutely outside, repelled, exiled, estranged, finally and unspeakably ignored."[7] They lost in their confrontation with God (Oedipal defeat).

It is possible to see in this story the childhood need for idealized perfection. Faced with Oedipal conflicts and the need to become independent and to rebel, children oscillate between shame over their own helplessness at not being able to make the world as they need it to be, and shame for their parents. Armed with fantasies of perfection forged in part by their parents, inevitably children turn these fantasies back on their parents, who fall short.

SHAME AND SIN: THE GARDEN OF EDEN

In portraying the story of Adam and Eve, Milton focuses on the envy, rage, and destructiveness of Satan, whose rebelliousness led to his supreme place among the profane, and whose consciousness of his shame and defeat is an integral part of his endless torture. Satan himself hates the sun (a reference to the source of light that makes seeing possible), explaining that he cannot escape himself, since he is hell. ["Me miserable! which way shall I fly / Infinite wrath, and infinite despair? Which way I fly is hell; myself am hell."][8] Profane and antisocial, Satan has no bond with God; he is free to do what he pleases and to cause mischief. Milton has Satan, unseen, slink about the borders of Eden, vault the thicket separating the Garden of Eden from the rest of the universe, land himself high in the Tree of Life and, from his elevated perch, attempt to see what he can. "Thence up he flew, and on the tree of life / The middle tree and highest there that grew, / Sat like a cormorant. . . ."[9]

When Satan's attempts to spy from the heights of the Tree of Life prove insufficient, he lands on the ground, adopting the shapes of different animals to get a better look at Adam and Eve.

> Down he alights among the sportful herd
> Of those four-footed kinds, himself now one,
> Now other, as their shape served best his end
> Nearer to view his prey, and unespied.[10]

The operative word here is *unespied*. As Satan sees how happy Adam and Eve both are, he is consumed with raging envy.

> Sight hateful, sight tormenting! thus these two
> Imparadised in one another's arms

The happier Eden, shall enjoy their fill
Of bliss on bliss, while I to hell am thrust[11]

Resigned to his status as fallen angel, quintessentially godless, never to regain his position in the Heavens, Satan shamelessly pursues his ends.

Squat like a toad, close at the ear of Eve;
Assaying by his devilish art to reach
The organs of her fancy, and with them forge
Illusions as he list, phantasms and dreams
Or if, inspiring venom, he might taint
The animal spirits that from pure blood arise
Like gentle breaths from rivers pure, thence raise
At least distempered, discontented thoughts
Vain hopes, vain aims, inordinate desires
Blown up with high conceits engendering pride.[12]

Satan knows how to threaten Adam and Eve's bond with God by blowing them "up with high conceits," "discontented thoughts," and "vain hopes, vain aims, inordinate desires." Paradoxically, Satan derives his power from rage over his defeat; God has cast him out for good. God won; Satan lost.

SHAME AND INNOCENCE

The story has been billed as about the "fall" from innocence. Yet on the surface it has little to do with innocence. Rather, it is about being driven out of an idyllic place by a disapproving God who does not like being challenged and who defeats the upstarts, a story expressing Oedipal defeat and shame. In the story of the Garden of Eden, disobedience and challenges to God's authority are punished and the authority of God the father reigns supreme. By contrast, in the Greek myth of Zeus, Zeus the disobedient son manages to disembowel his father Chronos and to take over the kingdom of the gods.

Milton has another take on the fall from innocence.

Nor those mysterious parts were then concealed,
Then was not guilty shame, dishonest shame

Of nature's works, honor dishonorable
Sin-bred, how have ye troubled all mankind
With shows instead, mere shows of seeming pure,
And banished from man's life his happiest life,
Simplicity and spotless innocence.
So passed they naked on, nor shunned the sight
Of God or angel, for they thought no ill.[13]

In losing their innocence (whatever that is construed to mean), Adam and Eve have understood how to dissimulate and lie. Now mankind can be troubled not with the real thing, but rather with "shows instead, . . . mere shows of seeming pure." *Real* purity is gone. And all because of "guilty shame, dishonest shame." For Milton the loss of innocence introduces shame over appearances, "seeming," and "shows." Despite snake and apple, it is not about sex, but rather about the loss of what is seemly.

KIERKEGAARD, DREAD, AND THE SELF SO EASILY LOST

Yet another perspective on the story of Adam and Eve is provided by Kierkegaard, who focused on the nature of the self and of the individual, and on the shame (for Kierkegaard, the "sin") which defines the human condition.[14] Kierkegaard realizes the conceptual difficulties in assuming that innocence is ignorance of sexuality. For him "real ignorance of the sexual, when nonetheless it is present, is reserved for the beast, which therefore is enthralled in the blindness of instinct and acts blindly. . . . Innocence is a knowledge which means ignorance."[15] In other words, for humankind innocence is not what it appears to be; because of its deceptive nature, it is a property of mankind only. Animals cannot be innocent.[16] For Kierkegaard, human sexuality implies consciousness, which in Durkheimean terms means that it always includes fears of being excluded (Oedipal anxieties and shame).

Interestingly, Kierkegaard wrote *The Concept of Dread* along with the frivolous companion piece *Prefaces* under the pseudonym of Virgilius Haufniensis, or the Watchman of Copenhagen. Implicitly, therefore, watching and looking have something to do with the notion of dread, and the notion of dread has something to do with shame, and with the loss of self,[17] Kierkegaard's terrible "sickness unto death."[18] Kierkegaard underscores the problematic notion of innocence, the fear of exclusion, and the importance of the social bond.

In focusing on the self, Kierkegaard relies upon G. W. F. Hegel's *Phenomenology of the Spirit* (1807), in which Hegel describes self-reflection as a process whereby one understands how the thinking self can be conscious. For Hegel, we "understand" through incompletion, through the forever inadequate efforts at grasping (and negating) who we are.[19] In criticizing[20] Hegel, Kierkegaard emphasizes the social context of consciousness and the moral context of history,[21] arguing that the meaning of history cannot ever be contained in any philosophical science,[22] that existence can never be described by an idealistic dialectic,[23] and that ethical responsibility (i.e., change) can never be accounted for within the Hegelian (or any logical) system.[24]

SHAME, DECEPTION, AND DESPAIR

The Sickness Unto Death set out to describe despair, a terrible anxiety, a sickness of the spirit, a "self disorder."[25] It was published six years before *The Concept of Dread*. For our purposes what is so striking about these books is Kierkegaard's determination to describe despair and its relation to shame, deceit, and the integrity of the self. For him there are three kinds of despair. The first is unconscious despair in which one is not conscious of having a self in despair; it is an illness that has not yet manifested itself, like measles before the spots. The second kind is "not wanting in despair to be oneself." When a young woman despairs over losing a lover, either to death, misfortune, or a rival, what she is really pained about is not being able to lose herself in him.[26] The third kind is "wanting in despair to be oneself,"[27] and failing.

Kierkegaard speaks of "the horror of this most dreadful of all sickness and misery, namely its hiddenness." And he continues, addressing the havoc and devastation that "hiddenness" wrecks, "Not just that someone suffering from it can wish to hide it and may be able to do so, not just that it can live in a person in such a way that no one, no one at all, discovers it. No, but that it can be so concealed in a person that he himself is not aware of it."[28] Like René Descartes and Hegel, Kierkegaard builds upon the Socratic maxim that the unexamined life is not worth living. "The only life wasted is the life of one who so lived it, deceived by life's pleasures or its sorrows, that he never became decisively, eternally, conscious of himself as spirit, as self."[29] To hide one's despair from oneself is to waste one's life.

The introduction of self-deception gives bite to Kierkegaard's descriptions of the total annihilation (i.e., disappearance) of the self, and provides a new twist to the Hegelian notion of negation.[30] When there is dread and shame over the instability of the world of appearances, the self must steer a course between imagining itself and recognizing necessity and limitation (i.e., the need for connections with other human beings). But the self can be knocked off course if it lacks "the strength to obey, to yield to the necessary in one's self, what might be called one's limits,"[31] or gives in to "fantastically reflecting itself in possibility."[32] It must navigate between narcissistic fantasies and a mortal dependence on others. "At a whim it can dissolve the whole thing into nothing,"[33] because of "something the Christian would call a cross, a basic fault, whatever that may be."[34] This feeling that what one is can, like Cinderella's coach, become a pumpkin, dissolve into nothing, makes a mockery of vanity and ambition in ways Pirandello describes so well. Related to Michael Balint's concept of the basic fault (1968), it drives the desire to disappear or reinvent oneself so as not to be seen as defective.

HE WHO SHEDS SHAME SHEDS HIMSELF

You will remember the organizing metaphor of this chapter, the Massacio depiction of Adam and Eve, eyes covered, being driven out of the Garden of Eden by an avenging angel. As the story of Adam and Eve illustrates, feeling shame, being deceived, and dealing with abandonment are basic human experiences. There is no way of avoiding shame, and if it is avoided, the consequence is inauthenticity, "all is but toys." In other words, it is human to feel shame (e.g., of a basic fault) and to need it to be communicated if one is to feel authentic.

To explore these dynamics of deceit, shame, and loss of self consider Pirandello's novel *The Late Mattia Pascal* in which self-loathing leads to deceit and deceit to a loss of self that goes unnoticed. The protagonist, Mattia Pascal, has always despised himself, his appearance, and his life, so he sets forth, leaving his lowly job as librarian in a small Italian village in search of adventure in the Great World. He wants to go to America, but gets only as far as Monte Carlo, where by gambling, he wins a large sum of money. Then, feeling guilty about his wife and mother-in-law, he heads back home. But as he nears his village, he reads in the local newspaper that a body was found in the river near his house. His wife identified the body as his.

Since in the eyes of his wife and his family he was dead, Mattia now had perfect license to extirpate "every trace" of himself, both externally and internally,[35] and to begin himself anew. The first thing he did was to transform his appearance: to get his beard and mustache shaved off. However, when at the end of his work the barber held up the mirror to him, asking for Mattia's approval of the work he had done, Mattia was filled with horror.

> In that first devastation I glimpsed the monster who, in a little while, would emerge from the necessary, radical alteration of the features of Mattia Pascal! Another reason for hating him! The tiny chin, pointed and receding, which he had concealed for years under that huge beard, seemed almost a piece of treachery. Now I would have to expose it, the ridiculous little thing! And what a nose he had left to me! And that eye![36]

In his horror, he concluded that with his clean-shaven chin he looked like a German philosopher. Some time thereafter, upon overhearing the learned conversation of two experts in Christian iconography who were speaking of Hadrian's beard, he decided to take his new surname, "Mies," from one of these experts, and precede it with "Adriano," something suitably Italian. He would have to acquire dark glasses and a broad-brimmed hat. Having thus clothed the persona he had decided to adopt, he set about inventing a new life.

However, as time went on he realized that he could not be satisfied or happy alone with himself. And then it occurred to him that he had invented Adriano Meis not for himself but rather for others, and that he could believe in this revised self only when others believed it. He was plagued by doubts over whether they did, since he knew his story had holes in it. Not only that but "this Adriano Meis lacked the courage to tell lies, to plunge into the midst of life." If Adriano was to live, for whom and for what would he be alive? Supposing, he says, that we have a musician and a piano. Now imagine that the piano is out of tune, that it has a few broken strings, and that it is not playable, so our pianist never touches it. If the piano is silent, does the musician cease to exist?[37]

Mattia comes to realize that, stripped of his name and identity, he is not freer, but rather ever more tied to what others perceive and want him to be. For all intents and purposes if he cannot be himself he really *is* dead. This point is driven home when, as Adriano Meis, Mattia falls in love with a young woman (Adriana) whom he manages to kiss, and who falls in love with him. But it is impossible for him to let on to her that he loves her. The love he feels he cannot express to her as a person he is not. He realizes that his freedom and newly created identity, at first limited only by a scarcity of money, have sentenced him to an unrelenting and diabolical punishment: his own company. "I had come so close to life that I had managed to pluck a kiss from a beloved pair of lips, and now I had to draw back in horror, as if I had kissed Adriana with the lips of a dead man."[38] Meis is a puppet with "a brain of straw, a heart of paper-maché, veins of rubber in which a little colored water flowed in the place of blood."[39] So Adriano Meis had to be killed, dispatched as a hat into which was placed the name "Adriano Meis," and dropped into the river. Mattia returned to his village as himself.

The price Mattia pays for murdering his connections with all those who know him is inauthenticity: he becomes a plaything to himself, a puppet, a clown show, and cannot take what he does seriously. He is a prey to Kierkegaardian dread. As Shakespeare's *Macbeth* says when he has murdered the king,

> For from this instant
> there's nothing serious in mortality:
> All is but toys: renown and grace is dead;
> The wine of life is drawn, and the mere lees
> Is left this vault to brag of.
>
> (II.i)

These lines recall those of Milton in *Paradise Lost* who associates seeming with the loss of innocence. The feeling that nothing is serious, that "all is but toys" seems to accompany an act so heinous that it makes the self unbearable, or, to borrow Sandor Ferenczi's expression, deprives it of shape or recognizability. Because he has murdered the king, the symbol of order, Macbeth cannot look upon himself, and because he cannot look upon himself, he is lost.

For Kierkegaard, "a self is what it has as a standard of measurement."[40] By murdering the king, Macbeth loses his standard of measurement, and thereby loses an essential link to himself and to others. Yet the loss of self, Kierkegaard notes, can and often does go unnoticed. "Such things cause little stir in the world; for in the world a self is what one least asks after, and the thing it is most dangerous of all to show signs of having."[41] Unlike Macbeth, the ideal self of Kierkegaard is implicitly a self recognizable by others, and, I would add, a self that carries with it the shame of human bonds, which can tolerate the anxiety of loss and therefore be free to enter into relationships.

As *The Late Mattia Pascal* reminds us, one cannot be overly ashamed of one's self without serious risk of losing it. Equally important, an ability to tolerate having one's self seen and recognized by others is a necessary part of having a self to hold onto. Too much unbearable shame leads to a loss of the self, and a loss of self generates more shame. And unconscious shame leads to greater dependency upon both what others see of us and what we imagine they see.

8 Narcissus and Lady Godiva

Lethal Looks and Oedipal Shame

> Under my gaze he turned pale; his form grew indistinct
> and his eyes a sickly blue—and finally he melted away. . . .
>
> —Sigmund Freud, *The Interpretation of Dreams*

Although the myth of Narcissus might seem to be self-evident, there are many overtones that give it particular salience for our time, and that relate it to the stories of Oedipus and Lady Godiva. Much of what goes under the heading "narcissistic injury" is, I think, shame based and related to Oedipal conflict. However, those writing on narcissism have tended to downplay Oedipal conflicts.

One of the reasons why narcissism can be so painful has to do with the failure of the ego-ideal[1] (the ideal of the self) to suffer comparison and to be allowed to live in the world. There is a terrarium quality to narcissism, like a child rocking himself to sleep because nobody else is there in the room. One way of defending against fears and experiences of abandonment as a child is to make a world of one-self. That is precisely what Narcissus does, and also what Oedipus does. But such defenses must simultaneously make the child aware of how little able he is to live in the world, to set forth to explore it, and to feel his own possibilities. Narcissus can be said to have made an ideal of himself, and then, unable to come out into the world (because the world was circumscribed by himself), to have made his ideal and himself one, to have disappeared into his own image.

In Greek mythology Narcissus is the son of the river god

Cephissus (Kephissos) and the nymph Leiriope. In one version of the myth, the seer Tieresias tells Leiriope that Narcissus will have a long life, provided he never looks at himself. You will recall that Tieresias was himself blind, having many times seen what he was not supposed to look at (e.g., snakes mating and Athena nude). Similarly, it was Tieresias who saw (and foresaw) the fate both of Oedipus and of Pentheus who died because he witnessed the sacred rites of Dionysus.

There are a number of variants of the story of Narcissus in which for many authors Echo is a later addition. Echo was the nymph punished by the Gods for having gossiped; Echo was never again able to speak for herself. When Narcissus became an adolescent, Echo fell in love with him. He rejected her, thus making the Gods angry. They punished him by having him "fall in" love with his reflection in the waters of a spring. He drowned, either by accident or by suicide. The myth links communication and looking; Echo can say nothing for herself and Narcissus can see nothing but himself. According to Pausanias, Narcissus needed to console himself for the death of his twin-sister, an exact replica, so he sat gazing at the spring to recall her features by his own. Narcissus is also the last flower gathered by Persephone before she was carried off into the Underworld by Hades, calling attention to narcissistic morbidity. In painting Narcissus is represented in the blush of youth, a "ravishing sight," as in the Caravaggio painting. If Narcissus were unsightly, it would be more obvious that looks can kill. Furthermore, Narcissus is represented as one at whom one wants to look, and who is unable or uninterested in looking back. So we as viewers can look at him freely.

In the tale of Lady Godiva, to which Freud also refers, she is a beautiful woman whom no one of the townsfolk has ever seen despite her habit of riding naked through the streets in broad daylight. To protect her modesty, all the inhabitants hide their eyes and close their shutters. However, one day a lonely man, surnamed Tom, defies the prohibition[2] and peeps through his shutters. This first Peeping Tom is punished for his ogle by going blind. In both stories, looking inflicts harm.[3]

LOOKING, NARCISSUS, AND NARCISSISM

All versions of the myth have Narcissus die. Yet, since to fall into one's reflection seems an unconvincing way to go, what Narcissus

actually dies of remains puzzling. Whether it is the Gods who punish him by making him fall in love with his image, or whether he
breaks a divine injunction by looking at himself, the result is the
same: he dies by looking. Since Oedipus puts his eyes out at the end
of the play, the themes of looking (and of being unable to tolerate
what one sees) are prominent in both stories.

But what is so dangerous about a look?[4] Thus far in preceding
chapters we have examined the look, both real and imagined, of others, the dependence on "looks" for a sense of orientation (as in
Pirandello), and the importance of Oedipal shame in forging an identity. In Narcissus we have one and the same person locked in what is
seemingly an invisible and deadly conflict. Might we conclude, with
Kierkegaard, that self-hate drives the loss of self, and that therefore
Narcissus paradoxically dies of self-loathing and disgust? Some writers imply that Narcissus dies because he sees his own poisonous look
reflected back at him. Gerard Bonnet suggests that what makes the
look deadly is the addition of the element of reality into what was
previously imagined, that Narcissus' imagination, however limited
and anxiety-producing, is less dangerous than reality.[5] Yet that does
not seem to give fantasy its due.[6]

In the light of the themes of this book, I can suggest another
interpretation. The boundaries between himself and the world being
therefore so fluid, Narcissus cannot see himself to be what he is not
by looking into another's eyes. Unashamed, fatally absorbed, and
enraptured by his own gaze, he falls into the pond and drowns. Narcissus cannot distinguish between his image and himself; there is no
uneasiness of shame that might prompt him to do so, no shameful
dis-ease to deliver him the confines of his own mind. Narcissus is lost
because there is nobody else in whose eyes he can imagine himself.
Therefore he disappears.[7] In visual representations of Narcissus (e.g.,
Caravaggio), we are drawn into imagining what he sees that we cannot. Oblivious to us, he "falls in." As Jean-Paul Sartre notes, it is
shame that keeps us human by imposing upon us our dependency
upon others; without shame we would disappear into ourselves.

There is another interpretation of the story of Narcissus: that
Narcissus dies of self-disgust and murderous, narcissistic rage. Like
Milton's Satan, Narcissus is unable to imagine how he could redeem
himself. When others fail to give back what the narcissist requires,
the narcissist, by negating them, cuts himself off from the social
world and thereby places himself at the mercy of himself. In Narcis-

sus one sees combined rage, fears of disappearance, and Oedipal shame (from which he retreats by negating not only triadic relationships but dyadic ones as well).

FREUD, LOOKING, AND
PSYCHOANALYTIC THEORIES OF NARCISSISM

Since the theme of looking figures so prominently in the myth of Narcissus, and since it is clear that there is something lethal about looking, it seems surprising that in his discussion of the subject of narcissism, Freud gives little attention to the visual meanings of the story. Similarly, in his discussion of dreams, despite their predominantly visual character, Freud quickly abstracts the motifs of seeing and being seen, although they are there in abundance in *The Interpretation of Dreams*. As Patrick Mahoney has suggested, although Freud developed the concept of a drive to look at (Schaulust), he never integrated this with his theories of narcissism,[8] although all the elements are there, and we will see how strikingly they are expressed in his dreams.

Let me illustrate my thesis that Freud avoids the psychodynamics of looking in his formulation of narcissism. In his paper "On Narcissism" Freud speaks of his theories of the development of the ego-ideal and of idealization. In the beginning, Freud says, the infant is his own ego-ideal, the ego-ideal being a substitute for, and representation of, infantile narcissism; it is the awareness of guilt—together with the concomitant moral consciousness—that brings individuals into the social world, weaning them from their infantile narcissism.

So far so good. But this account leaves out looking altogether, and focuses instead on abstract notions of energy invested by the ego in *either* the self *or* the outside world, an odd and unnecessary dichotomy. The picture soon becomes muddier still when Freud distinguishes between primary and secondary narcissism. "Primary narcissism," he thinks, is both healthy and inevitable. It designates a process in which the infant or young child invests his libido in himself. "Secondary narcissism," by contrast, is pathological, since it entails the withdrawal of the libido from objects in order to reinvest it in the ego or self,[9] thereby constituting a defensive regression.

But in viewing the selfishness of the infant as healthy and the self-preoccupation of Narcissus as pathological Freud runs into difficulties. Let us examine his text. When the child "is disturbed by the admonition of others and by the awakening of his own critical judgment, so that he can no longer retain that perfection, he seeks to recover it in the new form of an ego ideal."[10] Criticism and self-criticism would seem to suggest shame, but Freud avoids such implications, sidestepping shame and looking by focusing instead on the formation of the ego-ideal. "It would not surprise us if we were to find a special psychical agency which performs the task of seeing that narcissistic satisfaction from the ego ideal is ensured and which, with this end in view, constantly watches the actual ego and measures it by that ideal."[11] For Freud, it is the ego-ideal that looks and not the ego that is ashamed. Such a "measuring" function is, as I have suggested in earlier pages, characteristic of shame dynamics.

Furthermore, Freud turns his attention to idealization rather than to shame. That "perfection" of which Freud speaks is, it would appear, an idealized wholeness which he assumes the infant to have before the infant realizes that others exist separate from him, a curious kind of narcissism in which the infant disappears into himself because he has nowhere else to go. Paradoxically, in Freud's theory the selfishness of the infant serves the function of a lost Eden from which adults are excluded: they can never be freely preoccupied with themselves again. Nostalgia can never be what it once was.

Why, then, did Freud focus on idealization and leave out shame and the more obvious visual meanings of the myth of Narcissus? If looking is as pertinent in narcissism as I suggest, and as its place in *The Interpretation of Dreams* indicates, then why doesn't it occupy a central position in Freud's theories of narcissism? One partial explanation may be found in Freud's conceptualization of narcissism in terms of his economic theory. To understand the human mind, Freud's economic theory runs, one understands how and where limited psychic energy is invested. From such a perspective, narcissism may be defined as an "overinvestment" (or exclusive investment) in the self—rather than (and in opposition to)—the investments in one's relationships with others. Such overinvestment has a compensatory function, since it occurs in response to an experience that the self is lacking something essential. In sum, Freud's economic theory, in which there is a finite quantum of psychic energy to be invested, crimped his ability to explore the phenomena of looking and shame more freely, and to relate them to both idealization and conflict.

Between 1905 ("Three Essays on a Theory of Sexuality") when

Freud speaks about shame and embarrassment as affective responses to being seen and 1914 ("On Narcissism") Freud shifted to his economic model in which he "views" exhibitionism and voyeurism as defenses against drives.[12] The following year Freud published *Mourning and Melancholia* in which he relates narcissistic injury to mourning and loss, a subject to which I will return in the concluding chapter. In *Mourning and Melancholia* Freud suggests that what makes mourning so problematic are difficulties changing objects (i.e., substituting another person for the one who is gone) and giving up the bereaved because such attempts can so easily trigger narcissistic regression.[13] In the process of mourning, the bereaved has no choice but to change objects. Etymologically the bereaved has been robbed (bereaved comes from the stem *reafian*, "to rob"). But whereas in mourning there is nothing unconscious about the loss (one knows what has been robbed), in melancholia, there is an important unconscious dimension to the loss that is kept from consciousness by ambivalence. "In mourning it is the world which has become poor and empty; in melancholia it is the ego itself,"[14] and object loss is transformed into ego loss. Freud then points out that the resulting conflict between the ego and the loved person (toward whom there are unconscious hateful feelings) produces a split "between the critical activity of the ego and the ego as altered by identification."[15] This identification is, Freud notes, both narcissistic and regressive.[16] But whereas in mourning the ego comes to realize that the object is dead and gone, and comes once again to value itself and relations to other objects, in melancholia, there is a constant process of emptying out, an effort to kill off the hated part of the self that by narcissistic identification has replaced the object and which, now deprecated, disparaged, and denigrated, is, as it were, left to die. However, it cannot be gotten rid of since it has become a part of one's self, and becomes yet another cause of self-loathing and self-hatred.

To conclude my brief discussion of narcissism, let me review a few prevalent theories, none of which gives prominence to looking. For Melanie Klein and psychoanalytic writers in her school, the very concept of primary narcissism is misguided. Both Kleinians, and those belonging to the Object Relations school in general, maintain that object relations exist from birth; from their perspective the notion that one begins life focused exclusively on oneself misses the mark; the only narcissism for them is *secondary* narcissism that necessarily designates flawed object relations, an inability to rely on others.

A number of authors have associated looking and/or shame with developmental phases. Freud and Abraham recognized the narcissistic features of obsessional neuroses, linking looking, scopophilia, and exhibitionism to the anal period; Erikson (1963) conceptualizes shame and doubt as the affective consequences of problems in phases of development (e.g., the anal phase, holding on as opposed to letting go); Jacques Lacan (1949) maintains that the narcissistic or mirror stage of development is a necessary part of ego development,[17] an idea that Heinz Kohut and the Self-Psychologists would take up years later;[18] and more recently, André Green (1958) and Bela Grunberger (among others) have traced narcissism to prenatal states of elation,[19] making it biological and drive-driven. In *The Restoration of the Self*, Kohut, with whom the current emphasis on narcissism is often associated, explicitly makes shame pre-Oedipal. Although he does emphasize both narcissistic vulnerablity and the abandonment and injury of Oedipus, generally speaking he sidesteps Oedipal conflicts, Oedipal failure, and Oedipal shame. For Kohut, the absence of the expected response in the mother or parent triggers in the infant a wish to hide his needs, to be ashamed of wanting them gratified. As a result, the child becomes ashamed also of the inadequacy of his parents as well as of his own needs, leading to depression. But Kohut and the Self-Psychologists follow Freud's lead in not integrating a lust to look (and a fear of looking) with Oedipal defeat, and they assume that narcissism is essentially about deficit (however this is construed) as opposed to conflict. Even the distinguished *Vocabulary of Psychoanalysis* of Jean LaPlanche and J. B. Pontalis does not contain a single entry on shame, exhibitionism, voyeurism, scopophilia, or scopophobia.

NARCISSISTIC PAIN, LOOKING, AND MIRRORS

Persons exhibiting narcissistic pathologies are particularly shame prone. Not only are they unable either to communicate or successfully to hide or obliterate their pain, but they are embarrassed over feeling so easily wounded; they fear others will see how injured, defective, or vulnerable they feel. Despite being thought by others to be self-absorbed and criticized for not entering into the fray or being available,[20] narcissists are necessarily, although inadvertently, dependent upon others. What makes matters worse still, is their fear of

being found out: they often describe feelings of imposture, insub-
stantiality, and smallness, together with other painful shame-laden
feelings (e.g., fear of being seen to be damaged and pain over not
being noticed). In fact, narcissists genuinely *cannot* get their bearings
with respect to other people, in part because of the confusion of
boundaries suggested by the myth of Narcissus. Finally, narcissistic
withdrawal (disappearance and loss of self) is frequently felt itself to
be shameful, pointing the finger at some deep but unlocated flaw or
fault. Joseph Adamson compares Melville's Ahab with Narcissus.
Ahab becomes fascinated with his image in the water, and watches
"how his shadow in the water sank and sank to his gaze, the more
and the more that he strove to pierce the profundity." Ahab "drops
a tear into the sea, nor did all the Pacific contain such wealth as that
one wee drop."[21]

In the tale of Snow White, the mirror gives back what the
looker (in this case the evil witch) wants to see. And when it no
longer does, the result is murderous rage. Hence the dependency of
narcissists on mirrors. Only if the mirror gives back what they need
it to, can their rage be kept at bay. Yet their very dependence on the
mirror reveals to them that they are in mortal danger of disappearing, since they do not believe they can exist independently of their
image. As Ersilia says in Pirandello's "Clothe the Naked," she who
is everyone to others is nobody to herself. Consider a recent cover of
Newsweek depicting a scruffy little man together with his mangy-
looking dog as they look into a mirror, which shows them to be quite
different. In the mirror image, the man is a dapper gentleman, perfectly dressed in suit and tie, and the dog a thoroughbred.[22]

The essence of mirror-gazing is *imagining* rather than "seeing." As
Anne Hollander has noted, "that familiar mirror face . . . is always a
hopelessly private fiction: no one sees it but its owner."[23] In legend, mirrors are often associated with vanity and self-deceit, the self-delusion of
believing the false to be true. Images of "Truth" depict a woman with
a mirror, who holds it away from herself to reflect the light and the
world (shades of Plato again). She never looks at herself in the glass, but
rather uses it to see something that is not there (e.g., the past, the future,
and a different place).[24] Hollander comments, "In Renaissance art,
when a mirror is made into a little picture . . . the image is always a fiction."[25] Yet, even fictions are never quite what they seem.

In the mirror the look takes as its object the person and look of
the subject, a principal used with great effect by self-portraitists (e.g.,

Velasquez, Rembrandt, Chardin, and Picasso). The painting represents the painter scrutinizing his look, and trying to seize in his look something to express to others, these fictitious others whom he can imagine looking at his painting and at the image he has fashioned of himself.

LOOKING AND DREAMS: FREUD'S SELF-PORTRAIT

Let me now back up to the latter years of the nineteenth century, when Freud was working on *The Interpretation of Dreams*, in part as a response to his father's death. As I mentioned, in this work in which Freud looks at himself in his dreams (a peculiar sort of self-portraiture), Freud pays attention to the visual in ways that are, I think, useful to understand, particularly in the light of his de-emphasis on seeing as he grew older. Let me briefly review several of Freud's own dreams as these take up the themes of lethal looks and of humiliation.[26] In his "Non Vixit" dream, he is

> [O]vercome by strange emotions, I tried to explain to Fl (Fleiss) that P. (could not understand anything at all, of course because he) was not alive. But what I actually said—and I myself noticed the mistake—was, "NON VIXIT." I then gave P. a piercing look. Under my gaze he turned pale; his form grew indistinct and his eyes a sickly blue—and finally he melted away. . . .[27]

Freud thus dreams "Non vixit" (he did not live) instead of "Nan vivit" (he is not alive). Freud explains later that the "central feature of the dream was a scene in which I annihilated P. with a look."[28] The dream scene reminded him of a scene in which he (Freud) was the one to "melt away" before the eyes of one of his professors. "What overwhelmed me were the terrible blue eyes with which he looked at me and by which I was reduced to nothing—just as P. was in the dream, where, to my great relief, the roles were reversed."[25] On the reversal of feelings of humiliation, or on grandiosity as a defense against humiliation, it is pertinent to remember that Freud hoped to become a famous author by writing *The Interpretation of Dreams*. Freud writes,

> We may conclude that the foundation of the dream was formed in the first instance by an exaggeratedly ambitious phantasy, but that the humiliating thoughts that poured cold water on the phantasy found their way into the dream instead.

A number of Freud's dreams portray sensitivity to criticisms that he might have missed something, that there might be something he had not seen, a sensitivity that contributed to his use of the Oedipus story to convey the tragic quest of one doomed to pay dearly for his blindness. One of the best known of these in *The Interpretation of Dreams* is Freud's own dream of Irma. It is the very first dream Freud analyzes, his "specimen dream." The "Irma dream" begins as follows:

> A large hall—numerous guests, whom we were receiving.— Among them was Irma. I at once took her on one side, as though to answer her letter and to reproach her for not having accepted my "solution" yet. I said to her: "If you still get pains, it's really only your fault." She replied: "If you only knew what pains I've got now in my throat and stomach and abdomen—it's choking me. . . ."

As part of the background of the dream, it is pertinent to note that Freud had sent Irma to that unlikely and distant colleague, William Fleiss, a nose specialist. When operating on her Fleiss had unwittingly left a gauze in her nose. In a letter to Fleiss dated June 12, 1900 Freud describes the Irma dream. "Do you suppose, "he adds, "that some day a marble tablet will be placed on the house, inscribed with these words? 'In this House, on July 24th, 1895, the Secret of Dreams was Revealed to Dr. Sigmund Freud.'"[30] Might this be an "exaggeratedly ambitious phantasy" like the one referred to earlier?

Freud himself never had an analyst (or therapist) with respect to whom he could feel ashamed. But what if Freud used Fleiss as his imaginary analyst? What if one of the sources of the dream book was Freud's shame over tranference feelings toward Fleiss revealed in dreams? Thus, there is a "secret" revealed in year x, something that Freud can describe only via a symbolic dream. *The Interpretation of Dreams* allows him to turn his "professors" (i.e., parents and Fleiss) into people who melt away, transforming the omnipresent shame and fear of being seen to be inadequate into a compensatory wish to be famous. In this way he can retaliate against the professors humiliating him (recall also the remark of Freud's father, "This boy will come to nothing"), thereby turning embarrassment into the very principle of wish fulfillment. As Leon Wurmser comments, there is a shame dynamic in which "one who fears to be seen as weak [is transformed] into one who is seen and feared as strong."[31]

In one of the most obvious Oedipal shame dreams in *The Interpretation of Dreams* old Brucke dissects Freud's pelvis, yet Freud feels nothing at all.[32]

> The dissection meant the self-analysis which I was carrying out, as it were, in the publication of this present book about dreams— a process which had been so distressing to me in reality that I had postponed the printing of the finished manuscript for more than a year. A wish then arose that I might get over this feeling of distaste; hence it was that I had no gruesome feeling in the dream.[33]

We can only imagine what old Brucke was doing when he operated on this portion of Freud's anatomy, and we might expect Freud to feel some discomfort. However, Freud makes a point of saying that the "gruesome feeling" was not there. Rather than symbolizing humiliation, the dream becomes the fulfillment of a wish to be famous by writing his dream book; his fears of exposure are ascribed to his book, not to his person.

Also, if one considers the juxtapositions of topics in *The Interpretation of Dreams* as associative links, then it is suggestive that a particularly "revealing" section, "Embarrassing Dreams of Being Naked"[34] is immediately followed by one entitled "Dreams of the Death of Persons of Whom the Dreamer is Fond."[35] Given the death of Freud's own father (and Freud's feelings toward him) which prompted him to write the dream book in the first place, and given what we can presume to be Freud's feelings of unacknowledged Oedipal shame toward Fleiss, and given the prominence of prohibitions against looking that will become clear shortly, it seems significant that it is in this section that Freud speaks for the first time of the Oedipus story, describing it with exquisite sensitivity to issues of shame (and to what Oedipus could not see). The context in which Freud tells the Oedipus story lends additional support to the importance of my concept of Oedipal shame.

Freud notes[36] that the night before his father's funeral he had a dream of a sort of printed notice "rather like the notices forbidding one to smoke in railway waiting-rooms" on which the following words appeared: "You are requested to close the eyes," or "You are requested to close an eye." Freud immediately grasped the several meanings of the dream: he was being asked to overlook his father's death, and to close his dead father's eyes, lest he and his family be "disgraced in the eyes of those who attended the funeral."[37] There is also another obviously Oedipal meaning that Freud does not mention: closing his father's eyes can mean doing away with him, and being ashamed he wants to do so. Freud wants to get rid of his father as critic, much as the Lilliputians wished to put Gulliver's eyes out so he would not see how small they were. As Freud experienced his father's intolerance for rivalry from his son ("This child will come to nothing"), so Freud in this dream expresses his intolerance of Oedipal rivalry from his father (and professors), at the same time as he expresses fears of Oedipal defeat and shame.

Soon thereafter in the text, when speaking of nakedness in dreams as the symbolic expression of exhibitionism, shame, and embarrassment, Freud observes that "the embarrassment of the dreamer and the indifference of the onlookers offer us, when taken together, a contradiction of the kind that is so common in dreams."[38] To illustrate his point, he makes reference to Hans Christian Anderson's version of "The Emperor's New Clothes." Here, obviously, is yet another association to an injunction not to look. In this story, Freud writes, "two impostors weave the Emperor a costly garment, and all the spectators, intimidated by the fabric's power to act as a touchstone, pretend not to notice the Emperor's nakedness."[39] There are impostors, spectators, and something that is not to be seen. Moreover, in his discussion of the story Freud makes an astonishing observation: that disguise can take the form of an injunction not to see; that nakedness can conceal blindness. Here we are not far from the tales of Narcissus, who was told not to look at his own image, and of Lady Godiva, on whom the townsfolk were told never to cast their eyes. In all three instances, spectators who do not look are supposedly relied upon to protect the subject from being seen. Furthermore, the injunction not to look underscores the dangers inherent in doing so, and recalls the dream Freud had on the eve of his father's funeral ("You are requested to close the eyes"). Dangers here include Oedipal rivalry, rage, and fears of humiliation.

DREAMS OF TWO PATIENTS: A PAINTER AND A STRIPPER

Caught in an Oedipal struggle with his father, a painter dreams.

> I have had my head cut off. After a time I am told that it is back on because I can see, but I don't know whether it is or not. Then

I am overpowered by the desire to look at Picasso. I go up to his bedroom, but when I try to look at him, I tip over several of his paintings, and beat a hasty retreat.

As would appear to be the case with Freud, the overpowering desire to look himself, to decapitate Picasso-father, is reversed. Instead of having the Picasso-father-analyst decapitated, the dreamer himself is without a head. Essentially, this patient is being "requested to close the eyes," perhaps by removing his head. Like Freud's Non Vixit dream, this dream expresses a fear of being humiliated, thwarted, and belittled by his father, together with the wish to retaliate by doing away with his father so he could look freely. But once the dreamer tries to look, paintings are toppled and, by implication, damaged. Here again we find the theme of the lethal look. Might losing his head be seen as an attempt to defend against venomous looks, a defense against the Oedipal wish to retaliate against his father? And the wish to look at Picasso as a wish to be able to identify with his powerful father (analyst) and the wish to see behind the mask? As the dream ends, the dreamer is "forced to retreat," indicating shame over his impotence; the dreamer withdraws without the father's having done anything at all; he has defeated himself.

Consider also a vignette dealing with the Oedipal content of mirror fantasies, and the narcissistic regression from Oedipal conflicts. In her initial session, a woman now in her midtwenties recounted in a disconnected manner the following story. Several months earlier, working as a stripper with a different name and identity, she returned late to her parents' house having "tripped" on acid. She went to the bathroom to take off her makeup in front of a mirror, but struggled in vain to get the last bits off. Unable to recognize herself, suddenly she felt the mirror image released, while she herself disappeared into the mirror; where she had been, there was the mirror image, and she was now behind the mirror. Terrified and enraged, she went at the mirror with both fists. When she came to her senses, her hands were bleeding profusely.

How can we understand such behavior? One possible explanation lies with this woman's narcissistic rage and helplessness at being powerless to control her image and what she imagined to be her image as her mother saw (and hated) her. Intense feelings of rivalry toward her mother and Oedipal rage had led to severe splitting, in part to save her from unbearable shame. In the fantasy she is being shown by the mirror to be someone she hates violently, and at whom she lashes out. Also, can we not see this in the light of my suggestion that Narcissus killed himself because there was nobody else there in whose eyes he could be different from the way he saw himself? This young woman is trapped inside the mirror, and cannot get out.

What makes the mirror alluring is precisely what makes it deadly: the illusion it provides that the image *is* the self.[40] Caravaggio's Narcissus *is* his portrait, and nothing more than his image. Back we are to Narcissus, who falls into himself because there is no person outside through whose imagined eyes he can "see" himself. "We are lethal voyeurs," writes Salman Rushdie in his reflections on the death of Princess Diana,[41] a remark applicable not only to public reactions to O. J. Simpson and Clinton's affairs, but also to analysts themselves.

LOOKING AND THE TRANSFERENCE[42]

The stories of Narcissus and Lady Godiva have called our attention to lethal looks. Might the analytic situation and the use of the couch not be intrinsically threatening?[43] Are there not shame dangers exposing the analysand to the looks of the analyst while the analyst himself is shielded from the gaze of his analysand, out of sight but not out of mind? Freud did not want his patients looking at him. Might the analytic situation not be seen as a structural response to the dangers of looking and of Oedipal shame? Such a structural discomfort could, however, foster introspection precisely because it focuses attention on the "imagined self."[44] The analytic situation includes (1) the patient's fear of exposing previously unrecognized or unrecognizable aspects of the self (and/or family members and/or significant others); (2) shaken trust and confusion over perceptions and things not seen; (3) confusion (and shame) when the parent/significant other/parental imago/analyst proves incapable of being relied upon to relieve the confusion; and (4) Oedipal conflicts over feelings of shame, defeat, rivalry, and rage.[45] No wonder patients inevitably experience the analytic situation at times as dangerous. No wonder that analytic work takes so long, since having an analyst who "looks" threatens everything in a patient that has been condemned to remain unknown.

It would appear, then, Freud's references to the tales of Narcissus, of Lady Godiva, and of Oedipus can be linked psychodynamically. Lady Godiva needs to control what other people see of her (i.e., her appearance). Whoever looks is blinded. Narcissus falls into himself, unable to imagine being seen by anyone else. Oedipus blinds himself because of what he has failed to see; he cannot bear seeing others see him. Freud speaks of narcissistic regression as a falling into oneself, a killing off of the object in oneself, an expression of the most violent self-loathing that plays such an essential part in suicide and in the entire gamut of narcissistic and depressive states. Along these lines Ferenczi writes,

> The disappearance of one's own person, while others are still present in the scene, would thus be at the deepest root of masochism (otherwise so puzzling), of self-sacrifice for other people, animals or things, or of the identification with outside tensions and pains that is nonsensical from a psychological or an egoistic point of view. If this is so, then no masochistic action or emotional impulse of the sort is possible without the temporary dying of one's own person. So I do not feel the pain inflicted upon me at all, because I do not exist.[46]

With these remarks of Ferenczi in mind, if we return to the question, What kills Narcissus? there is another answer: unbearable pain. The myth of Narcissus cannot be understood without a consideration of psychic pain and the power of defenses against it. The intensity of obsessions about needing to be seen *in a particular way* would seem to suggest conflict rather than deficit (and conflict over deficit). The conflict-ridden final act of self-torture and banishment in Oedipus can be seen intrapsychically as the realization of his own fears, an imagined social response to his shame.

9 Of Fig Leaves, Real and Imagined

I could never tell a lie that anyone would doubt, nor a truth that anyone would believe.

—Mark Twain

Although it has often been assumed that the chief function of clothes is to afford us physical protection, and that shame and modesty are the result, not the cause, of dress (e.g., Westermarck,[1] Laver, 1969), it seems to me things work the other way round. Psychological, not physical, protection from exposure is, I think, the primary purpose of clothes. Clothes provide the illusion that we can "vest" our being, and by controlling the way we appear in the eyes of others, control our own feelings.

FASHIONING LOOKS, SHAPING SHAME

In *Fashion and the Unconscious* Bergler asks, Why is the half-clad more "alluring" than the nude? The question is all the more pertinent in view of the prevalence of writers who assume that "nudity" is "reality," that it is somehow irreducible, no more than the "raw material" that it is the purpose of dress to "fashion." But if, as I have argued throughout this book, what is most fundamental is the *imagined* appearance, the *fantasized* body image, and if this organizes what is seen, then nudity too is subject to the same dynamics of appearance as anything else. When compared with the nude, the appeal of the half-clad body leaves more to the imagination, and clothes (and fashion) are all about giving fantasy its due. If nudity itself were not subject to the dynamics of appearance, it would not be so dependent upon context, and consequently very different in the Nubian desert, the London stage, or a Boston living room.

Curiously, the relatively sparse psychoanalytic literature on clothes has missed the crucial importance of appearance fantasies and body image, and focused instead on exhibitionism. Freud's discussion of exhibitionism in the context of instincts and their vicissitudes (i.e., as a defense against instincts) has set the tone for the analytic treatment of the subject, much of which has focused on an abstract idea of clothes as defenses against the anxieties (e.g., castration anxiety) and instincts that are supposed to lie beneath them. Bergler, for example, suggests that women's fashion is driven by men's fear of women and women's bodies. Thinking about clothes in terms of castration anxiety, of fashion as driven by a fear of women, or by men's desire to make women modest to serve their own purposes holds out false hope of definitive interpretations. It forecloses further exploration, and neither adequately links clothes and body image nor includes a broad enough definition of Oedipal and sexual conflicts, leaving out what I have been describing as Oedipal shame: feelings of defeat, helplessness, and humiliation associated with appearance (including body image), conflicts over core identity, and sexuality broadly construed.

So just as nudity is not about nudity per se, so fashion is not about fashion per se. Nor is it clothes per se that make the man. Rather, the wearing of clothes in itself expresses an unstated conviction that we can "fashion" ourselves and our feelings, that we can make ourselves over. Psychic landscapes to be occupied by our physical appearances, clothes bolster the illusion that appearances can be made substantial, that the stuff of personhood can be as malleable as the stuff of cloth. Yet because this illusion makes others blind to what one does not want to see, it is structurally unstable.

FREUD AND EXHIBITIONISM

Freud's interest in exhibitionism was, as I mentioned, governed not by an interest in clothes or nudity or fantasies about body image, but rather by his theory of drives. In *Instincts and Their Vicissitudes*, he explicitly relates exhibitionism and scopophilia to sadism and masochism, reminding us of the destructiveness of looking and being looked at discussed in the Narcissus and Godiva chapter.[2] For Freud in this text, masochism is "actually sadism turned round upon the subject's own body." By extension, then, exhibitionism is the projected desire to look; instead of looking at one's own body, one has others do it for one. "It can hardly be doubted, " Freud writes, "that the active aim appears before the passive, that looking precedes being looked at."[3] Here Freud encounters a conceptual difficulty that he overlooks: with looking and being looked at, it is impossible easily to sort out active from passive, inside from outside.[4] The very experiences of "active" and "passive" would appear to depend upon the dynamics of body image, rather than the other way round. Remember my example at the beginning of this book of the mother who looks into the child's eyes and wonders (imagines) who she sees. In the back and forth interactions between mother and child, the child registers the experience of being looked at even as he looks at his mother.

Clothes can also express sadomasochistic shaming. Such "sartorial scurrility" can symbolize unconscious revenge directed at the shaming parent. Oscar Wilde, in his Bunthorne period, donned velvet cloaks and breeches in mockery (conscious or unconscious) of the clothes of his mother.[5] Similarly, in psychoanalytic work, clothes and appearance express much more than meets the eye. One day a patient who I had known for some years as timid came to my consulting room inconspicuously dressed but with his hair dyed an unexpected bright orange. I was shocked, but because I knew how shame-prone this patient was, I hesitated before bringing the matter up. The behavior expressed (among other things) both rage and an intense (and shameful) desire to be seen and recognized.

HOW CONSCIOUS IS FASHION-CONSCIOUSNESS?

While psychoanalysis has devoted some attention to exhibitionism, clothes, and body image, it has conspicuously neglected fashion. Why do women and men who obviously cannot *be* a model pay any attention to fashion at all? Fashion models transform the shame of inadequacy; rather than making us feel "less than," we can instead identify with the being whose perfection caused the shame in the first place (the reversal of which Freud spoke); we see what we want to see, imagine what we do not see, using them as an ideal, a standard of comparison.

Clothes in general and fads in particular express efforts to "fashion" ourselves, to "make" ourselves over in our imaginations and in the imaginations of those who see us. As Oscar Wilde noted, "Fashion is that by which the fantastic becomes for a moment the universal," that by which a shameful individual fancy becomes transformed. The history of sumptuary laws in Europe provides a clear indication of the perceived political implications of efforts on the part of those with money to "make" themselves.[6]

Paradoxically, then, clothes represent the visible without being what is seen in any reliably external, physical, or scientific sense. "The beginning of all Wisdom," says Professor Tuefelsdrockh in Thomas Carlyle's *Sartor Resartus*, "is to look fixedly on Clothes, or even with armed eyesight, till they become transparent."[7] Teufelsdrockh continues, "[T]he thing Visible, nay the thing Imagined, the thing in any way conceived as Visible, what is it but a Garment, a Clothing of the higher, celestial Invisible, 'unimaginable, formless, dark with excess of bright'?"[8] Without clothes, without the possibility that we can rely upon the illusions with which clothes provide us, we are, for Teufelsdrockh, essentially dead. Teufeldrockh's Clothes Philosophy, like the concept of body image, is based on the assumptions that a complete and harmonious sense of self is impossible; that identity is in continual flux, dependent upon circumstance and relative to context; and, above all, that what is of essential importance is internal fantasy life and the power to imagine.[9] Remember how, in C. S. Lewis's *Chronicles of Narnia*, the children enter Narnia through the back of a wardrobe.

Returning to the subject of models, we can ask, what kinds of fantasies do models lend themselves to? Freedom to ogle, it appears, depends upon making the person at whom we are looking into an object; the less personal, the less human the model, the freer we are to look; the more individualized he or she is, the more ashamed. Take, for example, the affair of Clinton and Monica Lewinsky. The self-righteous press wanted to be free to look at all the lurid details, the stained dress, and so forth, a "freedom" that required that Clinton be dehumanized, objectified, and treated as a freak. The greater the urge to stare, the stronger the denial that we are anything like him. And the stronger that denial, the more paranoid fantasies can take over. Mediterranean beliefs in the evil eye[10] suggest that looking can be experienced in terms of cultural categories of danger (e.g., Medusa and chapter 8 on Narcissus and Lady Godiva), and express culturally structured efforts to control such dangers. Clearly, then, fashion as "conforming" depends upon fantasies of where one is supposed to fit, the ways we seek to conform (or not to conform) to the situation. When the perfection of dress is desperately needed as a cover, and the dress or suit does not fit, it can only underscore the imperfections of the body on which it is being worn.

In her study *Outcasts: Signs of Otherness in Northern European Art of the Late Middle Ages*, Ruth Mellinkoff explores the iconographic use of clothes, hair, skin and appearance in the northern European art of the late Middle Ages, demonstrating how vital is the role of contrast and context in understanding vestimentary expression. For example, minstrels and heralds from the twelfth century on wore distinctive costumes, often parti-colored or dagged or both, indicating their low status by contrast to the clothes of the aristocracy. Yet patterned livery, first worn by people of low rank, had by the fourteenth century been adopted by almost everyone including the high fashion nobility, only to be demoted again in the fifteenth and sixteenth centuries as patterned dress became associated with flamboyance and as such despised,[11] as it was by the Protestant Reformation.

PLASTIC SURGERY AND CON-FORMITY

In our contemporary world it is striking how much technology feeds our illusions. People come to believe that an ideal of themselves can be actualized. Consider, for example, Nashville's Institute for Aesthetic and Reconstructive Surgery, the country's first all-purpose plastic surgery center. Each year thousands of people come to the computer-imaging center where "the designs they have on themselves are modified by, and electronically melded with, the designs now made possible by modern plastic surgery." There is actually a "Makeover menu." As Charles Siebert[12] writes,

> All plastic surgery patients are prepped in this way, turned into human contour maps—concentric circles, hash marks and arrows drawn in black marker to guide surgeons past an existing face, belly or thigh towards a more desirable one.

Joseph P. Rison teaches a course at Dartmouth College's Thayer School of Engineering called "Artificial People: From Clay to Computers." Rison characterizes plastic surgery as "the only surgery that's also a philosophy." In each of the "after" photos the subjects "bear slightly startled expressions, as though they have just crossed over some uncharted terrain." Plastic surgeons who fail to grasp the toxic shame that can be unleashed by their promises and skill encourage potentially devastating pathologies of appearance. Of modern technologies, few symbolize as clearly as plastic surgery how powerful is the illusion that we can control our internal feelings by controlling how we appear.

Consider also the "performances" of Orlan, a French performance artist and professor of fine arts at the Ecole des Beaux Arts in Dijon. Orlan has had nine operations since 1990, each one part of a work in progress called "The Ultimate Masterpiece: The Reincarnation of St. Orlan." In one operation she acquired the Mona Lisa's forehead, in another, the eyes of Gerome's Psyche, in yet another, the chin of Boticelli's Venus, and in another still, the mouth of Boucher's Europa, and in the most recent, the nose of a sixteenth-century Diana. The notion that it is possible to make one's person an "assemblage" of idolized traits seems to be peculiarly contemporary, like the Playtex slogan for women's underwear as, "Lingerie for Real Life."

However, through clothes selfhood can be experienced as something legitimate rather than feigned. Close enough conformity to a given fashion provides reassurance that one is not out of touch. Slavish conformity, however, reveals a shameful emptiness. When the model serves as a reminder of how despicable and hopeless one is, there is a natural tendency to want to hide, and an impulse to cover the hiding with shame, guilt, and self-loathing or, alternatively, an obsession with appearance.

CLOTHE THE NAKED

Pirandello's "Clothe the Naked" expresses the desperate struggle to avoid feeling naked and being seen as naked, with all this can symbolize.[13] Right from the start, the protagonist, Ersilia Drei, feels impossibly exposed and suicidally enraged, strung up before the public in whose eyes she finds it impossible to exist as herself.[14] As the play opens, Ersilia enters "as though she doesn't know where she is," stage directions that convey the feeling she is lost, lost both to herself and to others. One soon learns that she has tried to kill herself. Such initial confusion and disorientation persist throughout the play, growing increasingly complex and bewildering. Implicitly, Pirandello links feeling lost and disoriented to feeling naked, exposed, and ashamed—links I have made in other chapters. These feelings of exposure and disorientation, then, set the stage for the action to unfold, not unlike the opening of "Peléas et Melisande" of Claude Debussy and Maeterlinck (1902), both contemporaries of Pirandello (Melisande is also thoroughly lost, bewildered by a world she cannot understand. "Ne me touchez pas!" she sings repeatedly when she first appears on stage.)

The next characters to enter are Ludovico Nota, a celebrated novelist ("cold and thoughtful," one who "finds it difficult to make a real 'contact' with anyone"), and his landlady, Signora Onoria. Their interactions constitute a recipe for shame: Ersilia will turn in vain to Ludovico to know who she is; the novelist and writer Ludovico will inevitably misunderstand the disoriented young woman; and any sexual liaison will be frowned upon by the landlady, a prying busybody. Ersilia will try to find herself in Ludovico's eyes, and Ludivico will be embarrassed for imagining Ersilia to be other than she feels herself to be.

It soon appears that Ersilia has that day been brought home by Ludovico, who read about her story in the newspaper, and fancies Ersilia as his new partner.[15] "I never thought that the story of my stupid misfortunes could arouse the pity . . . of a man like you," Ersilia continues,[16] wanting the pointless story of her life to have some meaning, wanting to believe that the interest Ludovico has in her is genuine.

At this point Ludovico, misunderstanding, breaks in and interrupts. "You mean I should make it into a novel."[17] Following his own cue, Ludovico, in his role as novelist, begins to imagine what happened to Ersilia. But the results surprise Ersilia. "You imagined me. . . . What was I like? Like I am, like this? How then, Please tell me."[18] Mistrust gives rise, briefly, to hope, as Ersilia says, "Then *I* shan't be *her,* or *me,* but a completely new person." [my italics] But then this gives rise to fresh misgivings, "But I have never been able to be anybody."[19]

With increasing desperation, Ersilia seeks in Ludovico's vision of her some acceptable version of herself. But she cannot find one, since he continually misunderstands her, leaving her unavoidably ashamed of her inability to communicate some essential sense of herself to him, or indeed to anyone. In nothing she can imagine of Ludovico's (or anyone's) vision of her is there someone recognizable.[20]

Ersilia's predicament is impossible. Not only does she not know who she is, but she cannot identify with what anyone recognizes as her, and is therefore mortally exposed, psychologically stripped, suicidally enraged, and alone.[21] She has no stable internal objects, no persons in whose eyes she can imagine herself to have substance and continuity, nobody in whose eyes she can imagine herself to be "seen" as acceptable.[27]

Similarly, others become unrecognizable to her. Ersilia to Franco, her former lover:

> Because you—you can't comprehend what a horrible shock it is for me to have my life thrust before my eyes like this. . . . I am changed completely. . . . I see myself in that memory as a stranger, someone who is not me.[23]

As Ersilia comments to Franco, "My uncontrollable anger has been aroused solely because you so stubbornly refuse to understand me."[24] As shame breeds fantasies about oneself and others, so Ersilia must come to grips with how impotent are her fantasies. In this she sounds like shame-ridden patients, confused, enraged, and anguished at how they feel themselves to be different people, at how the analyst makes them angry by "deliberately" refusing to understand them. Such feelings intensify painful fantasies of how other people imagine one to be; one is helpless and cruelly "hooked" by the judgments of others (e.g., the analyst); one is at the mercy of others who can never be depended on to put oneself together; others make a mockery of the self one imagines they should see.

Unable to clothe herself in the eyes of others, Ersilia feels unbearably exposed, caught, and helpless. But her nakedness is more than this. It also stands for the need to deceive and lie, to scurry for cover (as in *The Rules of the Game*). At the end of the play, the dying Ersilia, who this time has taken a lethal dose of pills, addresses them all. "There, you see?" she says, looking at Franco and making "a small gesture with her hands that shows, without words, the reason why all tormented humanity must lie." Then, turning the tables on her tormentors, unmasking their attempts to cover themselves because she knows she is dying, she delivers her final lines, a meditation on lying.

> That's why I lied! Just to cover myself. . . . I wanted to make myself a beautiful dress . . . for my death . . . a bridal gown. But only to die in it . . . to die in it . . . that's all. . . . Just a little regret from all of you, that would have been enough. . . . Well then! No! I couldn't even have that! Strip it off! Take it away from her!—No! She must die naked! Uncovered . . . disgraced . . . despised . . . I never want to see or hear any human being ever again.[25]

In this chapter I have meandered from a discussion of the functions of clothes and adornment to plastic surgery and, finally, to the disorientation, shame, and rage generated by unbearable feelings of exposure. In the world of Pirandello, as with shame-prone patients, not only do people seem unstable; so too do actual events, which can neither be relied upon nor elucidated. Given basic discrepancies in memory and experience, "real facts" become far less important than the way they are argued about, than the anguish and confusion produced by disagreements. Having one's life thrust before one, recoiling in horror, not wanting to recognize oneself, being desperately ashamed of the self others see, and feeling violent rage at what others see—all lead inevitably to concealment and deceit that then fashion what is construed as reality.

The author Salmon Rushdie, condemned to death by Iran for his novels, writes of how he is trapped inside a metaphor, isolated in

> a bubble, within which I'm simultaneously exposed and sealed off. The bubble floats above and through the world, depriving me of reality, reducing me to an abstraction. For many people, I've ceased to be a human being. I've become an issue, a bother, an "affair."

But, unlike Ersilia, Rushdie can transform the pain of the simultaneous exposure and shame by telling stories.[26] Rushdie continues, "Those who do not have power over the story that dominates their lives, power to retell it, rethink it, deconstruct it, joke about it, and change it as times change, truly are powerless, because they cannot think new thoughts. . . ."

This is precisely what Ersilia cannot do because she takes her exclusion and nakedness too seriously; she cannot play with it; there is no embellishment possible. All she can do is rely on Ludovico's imagined version of her, a reliance that drives home the fact that she is nobody at all to herself. She turns to the other characters, but they never provide her with versions of herself that she can recognize. She is totally without adornment or defense, unable to clothe herself in the eyes of others. But she goes on anyway, trying to find in what others see of her something that she cannot find in herself. "And thus in modish manner we / In aid of sugar, sweeten tea."[27]

10 These Weeping Eyes, Those Seeing Tears

Trauma, Mourning, and Oedipal Shame

> Like the physical, the psychical is not necessarily in reality what it appears to us to be. We shall be glad to learn, however, that the correction of internal perception will turn out not to offer such great difficulties as the correction of external perception—that internal objects are less unknowable than the external world.
>
> —Sigmund Freud

I began this book with a description of the plight of Oedipus, who cannot see either his history (being abandoned by his parents and left to die) or his destiny (marrying his mother and killing his father).[1] Consequently, he acts out what he cannot understand, and his actions turn out to be disastrous. When Oedipus at last sees the destruction he has wrought, he is overcome with shame, and puts out his eyes.

The concept of Oedipal shame includes the mortification (note the etymology) of having had parents who tried to kill him when he was an infant, of having been stripped of a family, of having been alone and unrecognizable from birth. In response to such mortification, he acted out feelings of Oedipal rivalry by doing away with his father and marrying his mother. As I have suggested, Oedipal shame grows in dysfunctional families where conflicts between parents and children are avoided rather than recognized, where conflicts them-selves are often felt to be shameful and humiliating, where the child's shame for parental failures contributes to secrecy and to the child's omnipotent fantasies of protecting his parents, and where parental responsibilities become confused and compromised. In such families children come to repeat unconsciously patterns of defeat and humil-iation.

Despite pretensions to the contrary Oedipus is no more than a pawn of Fate who plays into its hands by trying to avoid it and who brings upon himself a terrible, mortifying sense of defeat. The Oedipal shame in the story of Oedipus is not only the shame of having been helpless to see, but also the shame of having, without consciousness, been abandoned and all his life unrecognized for who he is, a defect the recognition of which makes him utterly unacceptable to himself. Like Adam, what Oedipus does not know and will not see defines him. Tragically, Oedipus cannot come to terms with being defined by what he is not, since, literally, he does not know who he is.[2]

In the preceding pages, I have described many variants of Oedi-pal shame. Naturally there are many overlaps between Oedipal shame and Oedipal guilt. However, I hope to have shown that Oedi-pal shame has its own dynamics. As distinct from Oedipal guilt, which tends to call up anger, rivalry, and possible triumph over—as well as worthy protectiveness toward—the same sex parent, Oedipal shame calls up defeat, humiliation, worthlessness, and a wish to be invisible. The conflicts in Oedipal guilt (e.g., between hostility and protectiveness) have been well described in the psychoanalytic litera-ture, since they are easier to identify; but the conflicts in Oedipal shame, like the letter *A* embedded in the flesh of Hawthorne's dying Dimmesdale,[3] are more difficult to discern, involving as they do feel-ings of worthlessness, inevitable defeat, isolation, rage, and hope-lessness. Also, shame over flawed judgment raises once more the specter of human limitations. As Montaigne noted in his essay "on the uncertainty of our judgment," our judgments, like ourselves, have in them a large element of chance.

Oedipal shame can be excruciatingly painful. To avoid its pain, some go to the extremes of feeling and fantasizing invisibility. Yet such feelings of invisibility carry with them a conviction that one's feelings do not matter and are not communicable; once one feels fated to be invisible, the anxiety and isolation that follows can become unbearable, and one's worth undermined. One then depends on the expected, experienced, and fantasized blindness of others to hide one's invisibility to oneself.

Pirandello's characters attempt in vain to control the way they are seen, and are diabolically defeated in their attempts to be recognized; Alice cannot get her bearings from those around her, finds sizes constantly changing, and is defeated at the hands of the Queen, who alters croquet rules to suit her fancy and summarily wants to take off her head; Philby loses himself in his own web of deceit, and is threatened with defeat and humiliation no matter which way he turns (i.e., if found out by either the English or the Russians); in The *Rules of the Game* Le Chesnaye resembles his mechanical toys, boxing himself into a role defined by appearances; Jorieu will not conform to appearances as a hero and is killed; Milton's Satan, thwarted and humiliated by God who has cast him out, can only be bitter, vengeful, envious, and despairing, having lost any superego ideal of himself at all; Ersilia kills herself because she cannot feel seen by anybody and is unable to clothe her own nakedness in any communicable ideal, in a way not dissimilar to the end of Narcissus; Susan disappears when she cannot present to the world a face she can "see" and find acceptable; Sam dreams of feeling small in vast and large places, of being a lowly local overshadowed by large express trains; similarly, De Chirico dreams of his father in gargantuan, antediluvian images by which he is clearly dwarfed; unable to compete, Kafka's hunger artist fades away unnoticed and is replaced by a sleek, muscular panther; and Gogol's protagonists in "The Nose" and "The Overcoat" aspire to ranks and functions beneath which there is nothing, and which, when exposed, make a mockery of their feelings of total and abject insignificance.

REGRESSION, SHAME, AND TRAUMA: FERENCZI AND FREUD

I have shown how themes of Oedipal rivalries, conflicts, and shame show up in Freud's own dreams, and how Freud's preoccupation with aggression and guilt would seem at times to function in the service of the avoidance of shame and Oedipal defeat.[4] One example of these dynamics can be seen in his dealings with Sandor Ferenczi, who suffered from Freud's insensitivity to the underside of Oedipal struggles. Criticizing Freud for not allowing him to explore his feelings of "weakness or abnormalities," Ferenczi writes,[5]

My own analysis could not be pursued deeply enough because my analyst (by his own admission, of a narcissistic nature) with his strong determination to be healthy and his antipathy towards any weakness or abnormalities, could not follow me into those depths and introduced the "educational" stage too soon.[6]

Significantly, on July 21, 1932, exactly one month to the day before Ferenczi officially declined the presidency of the International Psychoanalytic Association, thereby marking irrevocably his rift with Freud, Ferenczi wrote the entry, "On the Feeling of Shame" in his clinical diary. Ferenczi anticipated with dread being defeated and then shut out by Freud in the struggle between them, which indeed he was. Several days later (August 27, 1932), Freud wrote to Eitingon that "Ferenczi's refusal [of the presidency of the International Psychoanalytic Association] was a neurotic action of hostility toward the father and the brothers, in order to preserve the regressive pleasure of playing the mother role with his patients."[7] From then on Freud essentially distanced himself from Ferenczi. When in September of the same year Ferenczi stopped in Vienna to read his "Confusion of Tongues" paper to Freud, Freud asked him not to publish the paper, and, as though to humiliate him by providing an unwanted pair of eyes, made sure that Brill was present at the meeting.[8] Subsequently Freud denied having done anything to injure Ferenczi, and implicitly viewed Frerenczi's sense of injury as further evidence that he (Ferenczi) was out of line.[9]

An instinct to cover up and to hide, shame experiences trigger defenses against *being seen* to be regressed, *being seen* to be traumatized, *being seen* to feel helpless, and so forth. Blinded to the dynamics of defeat and humiliation to which Oedipus had drawn him initially,[10] Freud could not recognize Ferenczi's Oedipal shame. Freud's narcissism (and his defense of his position as leader of the psychoanalytic movement) got in the way of his ability to grasp Ferenczi's idealization of him and to see Ferenczi's injury.

UNCONTROLLABLE EARS AND THE
SOCIAL-POLITICAL CONTEXT OF OEDIPAL SHAME

What is construed as "external reality" (read: appearance) can easily become used repressively to defend against internal feelings. The more internal feelings are repressed, the more individuals view their feelings with mistrust and the greater their dependence on appearance, the greater the tendency to mistake appearance for reality. Culturally, the loss of connection to our internal worlds has been disguised, misperceived, and denatured, rationalized as self-promotion, freedom, or independence, condemned as "alienation," "the me-generation," or "the culture of narcissism."[11] Complaints from patients of alienation, emptiness, soullessness, and isolation point to a disjunction between internal individual fantasies and collectively validated perceptions. For example, in the United States, the tragedy of the Vietnam War has been immeasurably more difficult to bear because those who fought could not easily strive for honor in battle; there was little external recognition for internal conflicts and strife.

One of the effects of shame is to crimp possibilities for communication and imagination. Unlike Rushdie, most people do not have a range of stories available to them. Appearance anxiety functions in the service of repression even in such unlikely places as the Disneyland phenomenon, where "imagineers" produce "fun" and "happiness" as realities larger and certainly more desirable than other feelings. By engineering environments, Disneyworlds repress human tragedy and helplessness, and reinforce an inability to feel pain.

It is interesting to compare the Disneyland phenomenon with the falsification of photographs under Stalin.[12] In photographs Stalin's political repression found its counterpart in psychological repression, an attempted defense against shame, and a sado-masochistic impulse to control appearances in general. Stalin, age forty-two, sharply criticizes the artist who did his portrait, writing, "This ear speaks of the artist's discomfort with anatomy," and again "The ear cries out, shouts against anatomy." Here we have Stalin offended by his ear, which he cannot very well exterminate on the principle "if thy eye offends thee, pluck it out." Similarly, Stalin has photograph after photograph falsified, distorted, corrected, or, if such rearranging proved insufficient, done away with. As redefined by Stalin, political necessity transformed the human and political landscape, "leaving holes in space, a seemingly inexplicable gap in a crowded row of colleagues." Drawings and portraits make Stalin look wise and glowing, overshadowing all others in importance, where in fact he is "small and cunning, pockmarked and swarthy, lost in the crowd."[13]

Stalin's outrage at his ear has led Tatyana Tolstaya to wonder why the ear should be treated as such an offender. First, she says, "We don't know our own ears," and don't generally see them as part of our image in a mirror. Second, "we don't control our ears. Unlike our eyes and mouth and hair, we can't change them with cosmetics or mustaches or beards." Third, as criminologists well know, ears are as unmistakably unique and individual-specific as fingerprints. Fourth, there is a Russian proverb about the revealing character of animals' ears. In a Georgian tale, a king grows donkey ears (King Midas also has donkey ears) which, out of shame, he hides under a scarf. Only the barber knows the secret and, pledged to secrecy, can tell nobody. Unable to hold the secret, he shouts it into a hollow reed, which sometime thereafter is plucked by a shepherd wanting a flute. As soon as it is played, the flute cries out the truth to the whole world. Not unlike the shame-ridden patients I have described, Stalin appears to have lived his entire life in terror of being exposed, a terror that drove his cruelty and sadism and that led him in uncompromising fashion to purge not only the past but, more ominously still, the future.[14]

APPEARANCE AND CONNIVANCES

The word *shame* goes back to the Old High German root *scama*, "to cover oneself." Shame is "a cover, a mask." *Schemen* in modern German means "shadow," or "ghost." Repeatedly, we have seen how the hiding of shame is about the shame of shame.[15] Even when partly successful, however, such maneuvers to cover feelings of shame are likely to alter neither their intensity nor the ways in which they are deployed in the evaluations of other feelings. Indeed, the implicit futility of efforts to hide shame from ourselves lies behind the etymology of our word *connive* derived from the Latin *connivere*, meaning to close the eyes. You will recall Freud's dream in which he was enjoined to "close the eye," conniving, as it were, with himself.

Thus connivance and self-deception are very close, both essential for an understanding of repression. When we imagine how others see us as discrepant from the ways we would like to be seen, such discrepancies resonate with discrepancies between what we feel we are and what we feel others want us to be. It is human to want to repress that "inward nakedness" of which Milton speaks in *Paradise*

Lost, particularly in view of the dynamics of ignorance, innocence, and deceit. Such inner nakedness and blindness itself needs to be imagined as recognizable if unconscious shame is not to be destructive.

Paradoxically we need our experiences of these discrepancies, of shame, in order to be sensitive to others, to battle against the forces of repression, and to be accessible to ourselves.[16] In this respect, narcissism represents an all-too-complete dominion of shame-as-repression which, if too effective, leads to the masochistic disappearance of the self of which Kierkegaard spoke. As we have seen repeatedly in Pirandello and in case examples, those plagued by pathological narcissism feel themselves in danger of disappearing, and come to rely on appearances in ways that cannot but negate their identity. Hence the intractability of the dilemma of shame; the more ashamed one is, the more ipso facto one depends on the idea one has of how one is being seen—and on those who are doing the seeing.

According to one female patient, if her loved one were only more competent at deception, there would be no need for her to doubt him, her disappointments could be discounted, and she would be spared the pain of not knowing who she is (i.e., she would not have to know she did not know). She felt a need to disappear so as to avoid the shame of feeling absent. Pronounced discrepancies between how one feels and appears to be perceived (either in reality or fantasy) inevitably lead to fantasies of disappearing. Better not to be perceived at all. Better to disappear, to die.

A BURDENOUS DRONE: SAMSON AGONISTES

Oedipus must come to grips with the full force of his shame at realizing that, having been abandoned as an infant, he could not see his own fate, and was ignorant of the process of his own undoing. Similarly, Milton's blind Samson Agonistes, more powerful because Milton was himself blind, must express his blindness, somehow make it visible to others. Yet to do so subjects him to the full force of his self-loathing.[17] Having "seen" his plight, the blind Samson attacks himself with withering contempt.

> Inferior to the vilest now become
> Of man or worm; the vilest here excel me,

> They creep, yet see, I dark in light exposed
> To daily fraud, contempt, abuse, and wrong,
> Within doors, or without, still as a fool,
> In power of others, never in my own;
> Scarce half I seem to live, dead more than half.
> O dark, dark, dark, amid the blaze of noon,
> Irrecoverably dark, total eclipse,
> Without all hope of day. . . .
> The Sun to me is dark and silent as the moon.

Sampson recognizes what he has done to bring upon himself such intolerable shame.

> let me here,
> As I deserve, pay on my punishment;
> And expiate, if possible, my crime,
> Shameful garrulity. To have revealed
> Secrets of men, the secrets of a friend,
> How heinous had the fact been, how deserving
> Contempt, and scorn of all, to be excluded
> All friendship, and avoided as a blab,
> The mark of fool set on his front?
>
> Effeminately vanquished? by which means,
> Now blind, disheartened, shamed, dishonored, quelled,
> To what can I be useful. . . .
> A burdenous drone; to visitants a gaze
> Or pitied object. . . .[18]

Reduced to nothing more than a shameful object, "a burdenous drone . . . a gaze / or pitied object," he has for himself nothing other than the contempt he feels from all those around him. "Thou art become (O worst imprisonment) / The dungeon of thyself." His shame is as unbearable as it is clear and public, visible to all as the shame of a once great and public man.

SHAME, DISAPPEARANCE, AND TRAUMA

Severe trauma triggers experiences of unbearable helplessness and fright. It is natural to react to these with shame, shame over feeling so helpless and shame for those parental figures who make one feel that way.[19] Better to pretend there is nothing, even if shame provides the only orientation to reality available. When others believe one's pretenses, there is a terrible hollow at the center of one's being. Fear of what others will see reinforces difficulties connecting with anyone. You will remember these lines from *Moby Dick*:

> Call me Ishmael. Some years ago—never mind how long precisely—having little or no money in my purse, and nothing particular to interest me on shore, I thought I would sail about a little and see the watery part of the world. It is a way I have of driving off the spleen and regulating the circulation.[20]

How we "drive off the rage and regulate the circulation" depends, at least in part, upon our ability to understand and work with our shame, to clear away enough unconscious shame to foster the work of mourning and loss. In instances of severe childhood trauma, the body remembers while the mind forgets, like the grin without the cat in Alice.[21] In defense the infant, who cannot tolerate feelings of vulnerability and dependence on one who injures him, identifies with the aggressor.[22] This identification with the aggressor serves masochistic purposes, as well as compensating for the experienced disappearance of the self. As Ferenczi notes, "the weak and undeveloped personality reacts to sudden unpleasure not by defense, but by anxiety-ridden identification and by introjection of the menacing person or aggressor." Therefore there is deep shame in the consciousness that this is what is happening, shame over the complicity which, unwittingly, the traumatized child has entered into with the very people responsible for his undoing.[23]

When afflicted by her eye ailments, Susan felt invisible because she could not see and could not imagine others seeing her. Her feeling of invisibility failed as a defense: it did not protect her. Rather, she felt her invisibility negated her existence. When Susan's counterphobic need to look was thwarted, she fell prey to early fears of total and abject helplessness. It would seem, therefore, that fears of disappearing draw upon defenses whose protective function has ceased to exist, or is experienced to be woefully inadequate.

Mark, who felt continually in danger of disappearing as a child, negated and "not-seen" by his parents, spoke of the relation between surprise and fantasies of disappearance.

Disappearance is about safety. As soon as you start jousting for a place, you get punished, a physical thing like banging my head on a car as I get in. A physical thing like being beaten and hit, hit very hard. Impossible to describe it in words. Very frightening. The worst thing about it is it comes out of left field. Always a surprise. If you knew it was coming, you could anticipate it. But it comes and is devastating.

Another patient dreamed in a manner expressive of terrifying neglect and danger unrecognized.

There was a child in danger in the street. The mother ran out into the street to save the child, leaving her own child unattended and uncared for. Then someone tried to calm the infant down, as it was very upset. The infant was in a sort of suit like a cat, but dressed up like the Statue of Liberty. However, although the infant quieted down, the person did not realize that by accident she had placed a plastic bag in the shape of a mask over the child's mouth and nose, and that the child was suffocating. She realized this, and took the bag/mask off. The infant was almost dead.

The mother does not notice that she places a plastic bag over the child's mouth, suffocating her. When she does notice, the child is almost dead. Images of the same sort abound in this woman's analysis, in which there are many things she does not, and cannot, see. One of the associations to the dream, preceded by weeping that she could not connect to anything in particular, came in the form of a feeling that she had never been the person her father wanted her to be, and that her mother never cared who she wanted to be at all. From the time she was four, she ministered to sick and ailing animals: birds, squirrels, and cats. As she grew older, her focus widened to include pigeons, chickens, and stray dogs. What her parents did not look at, she could not see, even if this was herself. The suffocating child had disappeared from her mother's attention and disappeared also from her own adult consciousness, so that she focused on saving animals without any realization that a dying child lay behind them.

With his customary style, Pirandello compares trauma to ripening by bruising. Fruits picked too early and carried to market are bruised to ripen them. "And this was how my spirit, still green, ripened to its maturity."[24] When a helpless child is mistreated and the suffering exceeds the bounds of the small person's power of comprehension, he comes to be *beside* himself, a state of "not-being," of having disappeared.[25] Childhood trauma troubles the outcome of Oedipal conflicts, leading sometimes to fantasies of psychic disappearance and to appearance anxiety. In his lucid and far-reaching paper on poise, Leo Rangell points out that poise is "a defense against being shamed, and unpoise a traumatic state of being shamed, of being despised, ridiculed, laughed at" and as such intimately related to being seen. Appearance anxiety in this connection, then, concerns the anxiety over whether or not one's anxiety over being seen as one needs to will become known to others. Rangell perceptively observes, "Patients with anxiety are often less concerned and tortured by the anxiety itself than by the question 'does it show?'"[26]

Maurice Sendak, perhaps best known for his *Where the Wild Things Are*, writes of his confusion when his mother would tickle his feet, even though (or rather because) he was angry with her. "Now I'm very ticklish and I couldn't stand it. I'd scream until she stopped. It was her constant pain not to understand why I didn't realize she was being affectionate."[27] It was Sendak's pain to feel that he was constantly hurting his mother when he himself felt hurt.[28]

AND A TEAR SHALL LEAD THE BLIND MAN

In a Freudian parapraxis that so well illustrates the themes of this book, Max Beerbohm told a story about his own school days in which a boy was to translate Euripides and came up hesitantly with the (altogether inaccurate) rendering, "And a tear shall lead the blind man." This line resonated with him, prompting him later to write after W. B. Yeats:

> From the lone hills where Fergus
> strays
> Down the long vales of Coonahan
> Comes a white wind through the
> unquiet ways,
> And a tear shall lead the blind
> man.

In concluding this book, then, I wish to emphasize the relation between shame, Oedipal conflicts, appearance anxiety, and grief. People for whom appearance anxiety, and fears of disappearing are prominent features of relationships have pronounced difficulty allowing painful feelings (e.g., of grief) to flow. The narcissist's inability to respond to the feelings of those around him chokes off tears and severely inhibits that mourning upon which the ability to bear loss and grief depends. Similarly, the inability to weep indicates some deep feeling of deadness, the consequence of cruel and ruthless repression as the primary defense against trauma and the shame of being seen to be injured. Mattia Pascal wanted to remove every trace of himself; he went to have his beard and mustache shaved off, to symbolize the transformation. Grieving and mourning, together with an understanding of Oedipal conflicts and shame dynamics and the ways in which they increase reliance on appearance are, I think, essential in working through toxic shame cycles. Correspondingly, failure to mourn intensifies not only toxic shame but also rage, despair, appearance anxiety, and shame-driven sadomasochistic cycles, which in public figures like Hitler or Stalin can cause incalculable devastation.

The more powerful the fantasies to control appearances (e.g., Stalin's photographs), the stronger the need to control feelings; the more cruelly repressive the forces at work against mourning, and the more intolerant one's own standards of who one is, the more one sets *others* up so they can be experienced as repressive (e.g., spouses or mates who can be relied upon to function repressively). In other words, the more one will depend on others not to understand whatever feelings one finds unacceptable in oneself. Ersilia relies upon the others not to see her, so she does not have to see herself. When she does reveal herself, she knows she is dying and does so in rage, defiance, and despair. Susan broke down when she could not control the way she appeared, and found herself looking in the mirror at one without a face. Sam, who had abandoned hope of controlling his appearance, fantasized being invisible so no one could see him in an unfavorable light, or a spy, a triple agent nobody could identify. There is, however, the other side to shame dynamics. As Wurmser notes, shame can also bring about heroic transcendence.

As a bookend to the Oedipus story, let me conclude with these lines from Andrew Marvell,[29] for whom being able to weep is being able to see:

How wisely Nature did decree,
With the same eyes to weep and see!
That, having viewed the object vain,
We might be ready to complain. . . .

Ope then, mine eyes, your double sluice,
And practice so your noblest use,
For others too can see, or sleep,
But only human eyes can weep. . . .

Thus let your streams o'erflow your springs,
Till eyes and tears be the same things:
And each the other's difference bears;
These weeping eyes, those seeing tears.

Notes

1. Building on the clinical work of H. B. Lewis (1971), Piers and Singer (1953), Wurmser (1981, 1987), Schneider (1977), and Tomkins (1962, 1963, 1991) on the one hand, and on the other hand socially oriented writers like Benedict (1946), Doi (1973), and Lynd (1958), writers of the last decade have vigorously explored the subject of shame from various perspectives. Morrison (1989, 1996) and Broucek (1991), adopting an approach inspired by self-psychology, have explored shame in its relation to narcissism, as protection against narcissistic wounding, and as the expression of deficit and defect. Lansky (1992, 1996, 1997) has adopted a more clearly conflict-based approach informed by family dynamics. Rizzuto (1991) has explicitly emphasized unconscious conflict. M. Lewis (1992) has provided a useful overview. Nathanson (1987), following in the tradition of Tomkins, has emphasized shame as an individual product of biological hard-wiring. Bringing legal expertise to bear, Miller (1993) approaches shame as a socially constructed consequence of failed reciprocity. From philosophy come writers like Wollheim (1999), who focuses on the "so-called moral emotions"(a concept borrowed from eighteenth-century writers like Adam Smith) and Williams (1993), who emphasizes shame as a basis for responsibility and moral judgments. From literature Adamson (1997) takes up shame in the work of Melville (1988) and others, and Clark (1999) writes of Sexton's shame. From sociology, Goffman (1959) has written about the presentation of self in everyday life, and Scheff and Retzinger (1991) have stressed the social value of fears of exclusion (and shame over being excluded). Of the review essays on a range of books in different disciplines, see, for example, Kilborne 1995a, 1997.

2. See Lansky (1996) on the shame-based rage and suicide of Ajax.

3. See, for example, the classic paper of Bion (1959) dealing with attacks on linking.

133

4. See, for example, *Civilization and Its Discontents* (1930) in which Freud explains that because sexual and aggressive drives can override all other concerns, civilization depends upon guilt and repression. In this text, Freud holds that the socializing emotion in the face of aggression is guilt, and scarcely mentions shame and feelings of defeat at all.

5. As should be clear implicitly, the literature on Object Relations is also indispensable for an understanding of shame dynamics.

6. Not only do mother and child imagine seeing when they look, smelling when they smell, but they use cross-sensory fantasies: when they see, they imaging listening, when they hear, imagine touching, when they touch, imagine smelling, and so forth. See, for example, Brazelton, Koslowski, and Main (1974), Novick and Novick (1991, 1992), and Weissman (1977). The work of Spitz (1950, 1957, 1965) remains a baseline.

7. Merleau-Ponty (1964) and the phenomenologists in general attempt an analysis of self-experience that by definition defies Cartesian logic. The methods they use rely upon Hegel's notions of negation and dialectic. Hegel (1807) and Sartre (1964, 1975, 1983) both explicitly deal with self-consciousness as a feeling and not simply as "objective" knowledge; both aim at describing phenomena underlying rationalization; both aim at analyzing interpersonal processes by casting aside the usual logical formulas; and both believe that truth belongs to what is known of the self not in isolation (e.g., Kant, 1781, 1790), but rather in relationship to others. However, both tend to reduce the irrational to something rationally comprehensible. "It is easier to manufacture seven facts than one emotion," quipped Twain.

8. See, for example, Devereux (1972, 1976, 1980), one of the few writers who has sought to describe observation with epistemological sophistication.

9. See, for example, Kilborne (1992a). It is natural for one who looks to want to "not see," to "not know" that he is seen to be looking, since emotions are far more difficult to describe than behaviors. In psychoanalysis, one current trend has been pursued by Renik (1995, 1996, 1998) and others. Renik has sought to describe the "perils of neutrality" making much the same point as Devereux about the necessary and inevitable effects of observer on the observed. Speaking of unobjectionable countertransference, Fox (1998) and others have widened the field of inquiry.

10. Mauss (1967, p. 38).

11. Derida writes, "Toute notre philosophie est une photologie. La metaphore de l'ombre et de la lumière (de se montrer et de se cacher) (est) la métaphore fondatrice de la philosophie occidentale comme meta-

physique." "All our philosophy is a photology. The metaphor of shadow and light (revealing and hiding) is the fundamental metaphor of Occidental philosophy as metaphysics" (1967, p. 45) [my translation]. Generally speaking, there is far more literature on looking in French than there is in English. Derida was given free reign by the Louvre to organize an exhibition (Memoires d'aveugle) in 1990–1991 that yielded a catalogue (1990). One of the best-known French texts on the subject of blindness is that of Diderot, *Lettres aux aveugles à l'usage de ceux qui voient* (Letters to the blind for those who see). Two other works that come to mind are those of Vernant (1985) in Classics and Starobinski (1961) in Literature. The blindness of Oedipus is all the more striking since it has as its foil the prophecy of the blind Teiresias, who knew but could not see.

12. For the essence of Plato's theories of the visible and the invisible, see the *Phaedo,* pp. 79ff. and the *Republic*, pp. 6.509dff.

13. When "seeing is believing" (a basic assumption of certain skeptical positions) our Greek rationalist (Platonic) tradition converges with our Judeo-Christian tradition (e.g., the light of God) in reinforcing the connections between seeing and understanding. Specifically, when Plato (e.g., *The Republic*) distinguishes between "the visible" and the "intelligible," the processes of sight and insight remain conceptually comparable. Berenson observes, "representation is a compromise with chaos whether visual, verbal or musical" (1953, p. 27).

14. Painters like Correggio, following in Leonardo's tradition, sought to make the invisible visible. As Zimmer (1997) has recently written, Correggio "had the perseverance as well as the genius needed to make a fictitious world of dreams seem real." Zimmer refers to Correggio's painting of Io (now in Vienna) in which as a cloud Jupiter embraces a nymph. "It makes you feel that you actually see the impossible happen in front of you."

15. For an investigation of the ways in which our peceptions of scientific problems in the social sciences affect our theories see Devereux(1976a). Speaking of the visual arts, Berenson writes that they combine what we see and what we know (and also what we don't see and what we don't know) (1953, p. 37).

16. But a useful question to ask is, closure of what? Here it would appear that the "what" (whatever it is) is a sense of bodily self organized around some *fantasized* center (see, e.g., Bloomer and Moore, 1977, pp. 39ff.). Beginning just before the First World War, the Berlin school of Gestalt (form) psychologists demonstrated that our rational perception takes place against a background of irrational experiences tending to "organize" what we perceive in ways of which we are not conscious.

17. "Faire une phénomenologie de l'autre monde comme limite d'une phénomenologie de l'imaginaire et du 'caché'. Quand je dis donc que tout visible est invisible, que la perception est imperception, que la conscience a un "punctum caecum," que voir c'est toujours voir plus qu'on ne voit—il ne faut pas le comprendre dans le sens d'une contradiction. Il ne faut pas se figurer que j'ajoute au visible . . . un non-visible. Il faut comprendre que c'est la visibilité même qui comporte une non-visibilité" (Merleau-Ponty, 1964, p. 300). [I strive] to make a phenomenology of the other world as the limit of the phenomenology of the imaginary, of the hidden. When I say that everything that's visible is invisible, that perception is imperception, that consciousness has a *puctum caecum*, that to see is always to see more than one sees—one must not understand this as a contradiction. Do not imagine that I am adding to the visible something not visible. Rather it is visibility itself that includes nonvisibility. [my translation]

18. Consider the image of Justice with a blindfold. Might the conflicts hidden by the blindfolds of Justice arise from conflicting claims of reason and of the heart? What of the blindness of Love? If both love and justice are imagined to be sightless, then of what use is reason? Perhaps love is blind to the defects of the individual in question, saving the loved one from the shame of feeling flawed (and the lover from the shame of loving one who is flawed).

CHAPTER ONE

1. The concepts of psychic size and of size anxiety have been adumbrated in an earlier paper (Kilborne, 1996) which constitutes an independent version of material in this chapter.

2. "In the first place self-regard appears to us to be an expression of the size of the ego; what the various elements are which go to determine size is irrelevant. Everything a person possesses or achieves, every remnant of the primitive feeling of omnipotence which his experience has confirmed, helps to increase his self-regard" (Freud, 1914a, p. 98).

3. Arnheim (1955, p. 218).

4. Edelstein and Edelstein (1945).

5. Upness is extremely important as a part of our haptic sense. Arnheim, in a section of *The Dynamics of Architectural Form* entitled "Vision Takes to the Upright," explains that it is the vertical plane we perceive and use in organizing our perceptions, and that "no direction along the ground plane is spatially distinguished" (1977, p. 35). Interestingly, then, our sense of hierarchy, of upness and downness that influences our perceptions of body height and "psychic size," can be related to more general notions of spatial orientation.

6. When speaking of body image and its relation to architecture and memory, Bloomer and Moore emphasize a concept that is psychological rather than physical. They define body image as "the complete feeling, or three-dimensional Gestalt (sense of form) that an individual carries at any one moment in time, of his spatial intentions, values, and his knowledge of a personal, experienced body" (1977, p. 37).

7. There are many kinds of differences that could be described here, most obviously sexual differences, the way in which women tend to be objectified and "seen" differently from men. But my emphasis here is on the process of comparison and the dynamics of whatever is taken to be the fantasized standard.

8. For Merleau Ponty (1964), perception is what goes on inside a cognizing subject to represent what exists outside itself. See, for example, Madison in Busch and Gallagher (1992, p. 84).

9. Schilder (1950, p. 11).

10. Schilder writes (1950), "The image of the body is constructed," continually tested "to find out what parts fit the plan and fit the whole. . . . The body image is, to put it in a paradoxical way, never a complete structure; it is never static: there are always disrupting tendencies" (pp. 286–287).

11. Swift, *Gulliver's Travels* (1726, p. 124).

12. Ibid., p. 125.

13. Ibid.

14. *New York Times*, December 29, 1995.

15. Ferenczi (1926, p. 55). Ferenczi's paper on Gulliver Fantasies picks up on themes of humiliation. With his usual sense of irony and fun, Ferenczi gave this paper when invited to deliver a lecture in the United States. He came from a small and relatively unknown country (Hungary) to speak to more prominent colleagues in a powerful place.

16. In her book *Swift and Carroll: A Psychoanalytic Study of Two Lives* (1955), Phyllis Greenacre stresses the implications of size instability for identity, and points out some of the similarities in psychodynamics between Swift and Carroll.

17. As I have discussed elsewhere (Kilborne, 1998a), Ferenczi's Gulliver text, "shrinks" his rival Rank and diminishes the importance of his theories of birth trauma in an effort to define more satisfactorily the nature of trauma and also to secure his place as the father's (Freud's) favorite son. In his Gulliver text, which focuses on Swift's absent father and the difficulty he

has in working through his Oedipal conflicts, Ferenczi would seem to be speaking of a similar feeling toward an insufficiently available Freud, toward whom he is unable to express and work through competitive, negative feelings. These are, it is to be remembered, features of Ferenczi's Gulliver paper that presumably are called forth by its subject matter, and deal with rivalry, competition, rage, and hostility and, of particular significance for this book, feelings of Oedipal defeat and humiliation. On the Freud-Ferenczi relationship, see, for example, Bergmann (1997); Bokanowski (1996, 1998); Bonomi (1999); Brabant, Falzeder, and Giampieri-Deutsch (1992); Dupont (1994); Haynal (1997); Hoffer (1985, 1997); Kirschner (1993); and Martin-Cabré (1997).

18. She had dreams of being small:

I am in a house, the rooms of which are arranged in a row such that you have to go through some to get to the others. I live in this house with my mother and maternal grandmother and my sister. My mother and grandmother are not there, and my sister is asleep on one of the trapazoidal beds in the house. I am in the middle room trying to cheer up a little girl about six years old staring off into space, just looking at the walls. She is not as cute as I was, but she seems to be me in the dream.

Associations included not knowing she was lonely because she did not know what loneliness was, and persistent feelings of smallness, isolation, and muted sadness when growing up. It was extremely difficult to get her to express feelings of loneliness in my presence.

19. For years, when she looked in vain to significant others to reassure her that she was important to them, she would feel she was shrinking, a theme repeated continually in the transference during the analysis.

20. Differences in size between the two of us were used in fantasy by this patient to confirm fears that being a woman means submitting to the man in the most humiliating and degrading fashion. The negative value she attributes to her littleness constitutes another reminder of the importance of Freud's observation that the ego is first and foremost a body ego, and that the body ego is experienced in terms of how one feels about one's self.

21. Quoted in Armstrong (1990, p. 415).

22. My discussion of smallness in Dickens is based on Armstrong, "Gender and Miniaturization: Games of Littleness in Nineteenth Century Fiction" *English Studies in Canada*, 16 (4) 1990. This paper concentrates on miniaturization in the representations of women.

23. *Sketches of Young Couples* (Dickens, 1840).

24. *Our Mutual Friend* (Dickens, p. 268), quoted in Armstrong (p. 406).

25. See Shorter (p. 66), quoted in Armstrong (1990, p. 414).

26. John Updike's foreword to *Franz Kafka The Complete Stories* (1971, p. xvii).

27. Updike (1971, p. xxi).

28. Swift (1726, p. 146).

29. According to van der Velde, body images contribute substantially to a sense of personal identity. "They enable man to project how others see him by means of his appearances," to preserve "a desirable view of himself; and they enable him to create within others impressions that do not precisely reflect his actual self" (1985, p. 527).

30. While shooting *Sante Fe Trail*, Errol Flynn insisted on being more prominent than anyone else and displaced the young Ronald Reagan, whom he believed was getting too much of the foreground. Reagan countered by covertly making a mound of dirt to stand on, so he was distinctly taller than his rival.

31. Baxter (1993, p. 147).

32. Ferenczi (1985, pp. 128–129).

33. Rangell (1953, p. 6).

34. Compare the following dream of the painter De Chirico:

In vain I struggle with a man whose eyes are shifty and very gentle. Each time that I get him in my grip, he frees himself by gently spreading his arms; his arms are unimaginably strong: they are like irresistible levers, gigantic cranes which rise above the swarming shipyards, floating fortresses with towers heavy as the breasts of antediluvian mammals. In vain I struggle with the man of gentle looks who eyes me suspiciously: from each hold, no matter how strong, he frees himself gently, smiling, by hardly spreading his arms. . . . The struggle ends in my giving in: I give up; then the images blur: the river (the Po or the Penee) which during the struggle I knew flowed close to me, darkens; the images intermix as though storm clouds were hovering overhead; there is an intermezzo during which I am perhaps still dreaming, but I remember nothing, only agonizing quests along darkened streets. The dream lights up again. I find myself on a piazza of great metaphysical beauty. . . . I look toward the hills over which loom the last clouds of the fleeing storm; here and there the villas are all white with something tomb-like and solemn about them when seen against the deep black curtain of the sky. All at once I find myself under the portico amongst a group of people who jostle one another at the door of a pastry shop, the shelves of which are stacked with multicolored cakes; people crowd around and look inside, as they do at the door of a pharmacy when an injured or sick passerby is brought in from the street; but while looking inside, I see my father from behind, standing in the middle of the pastry shop, eating a cake; yet I do not know whether it is for him that people are crowding at the door; a certain anxiety then comes over me and I want to flee towards the west, a new, more hospitable land. At the same time I fumble in my clothes for a dagger, because it seems to me that my father is in danger in this pastry shop and I feel that if I go in, I would need a weapon as when one enters the lair of thieves. My anxiety grows. Suddenly the crowd presses in on me and carries me towards the hills; I have the impression that my father is no longer in the pastry shop, that he has fled, that he is going to be pursued like a thief and I waken in anxiety over this thought. Quoted in Kilborne and Degarrod (1983).

CHAPTER TWO

1. Pirandello (1952, pp. 379–380).

2. Pirandello (1988, p. 24).

3. The French word *réaliser* means at once "realize" and "stage," "recognize," and "put on" (as a play is put on).

4. Pirandello (p. 36).

5. Ibid., p. 65.

6. "I am the son of Chaos," Pirandello wrote of himself, "not allegorically but literally, because I was born in a country spot, called, by the people around, *Cavasu*, a dialectal corruption of the authentic, ancient Greek word, *chaos*" (Bentley, 1946, p. 79). For him, life is chaotic, unstable, constantly in flux; he *is* chaos.

7. Updike (1971, p. xvii).

8. An allusion to Rilke's *Notebooks of Malte Laurids Brigge*.

9. Quoted by Adler (*New York Review of Books*, October 18, 1997). In his Weltinnenraum poem Rilke writes, "in you stands your father/and stares." Describing feelings of Oedipal shame and referring to Malte, Rilke writes in his *Letters on Cezanne*,

And suddenly (and for the first time) I understand the fate of Malte Laurids. Isn't it this: that this testing by the real exceeded his capacities, that he failed, even though in his mind he was so convinced of the need for this testing that he instinctively sought it out until it embraced him and clung to him and never left him again? The book of Malte Laurids, once it is written, will be but the book of this realization, proven in the failure of one for whom it was too vast, too great. And perhaps he passed the test, after all: for he wrote the death of the chamberlain; but like Raskolnikov he was left behind, used up by his deed, ceasing to act at the moment that called for action to begin, so that his new, hard-gained freedom turned against him and, finding him defenseless, tore him to pieces. (1985, p. 69)

10. Quoted in Wurmser (1981).

11. Consider in this context the well-known passage from *Mourning and Melancholia*.

The object-cathexis proved to have little power of resistance and was brought to an end. But the free libido was not displaced on to another object: it was withdrawn into the ego. There, however, it was not employed in an unspecified way, but served to establish an identification of the ego with the abandoned object. Thus the shadow of the object fell upon the ego, and the latter could henceforth be judged by a special agency, as though it were an object, the forsaken object. In this way an object-loss was transformed into an ego-loss and the conflict between the ego and the loved person into a cleavage between the critical activity of the ego and the ego as altered by identification. (Freud, 1915, p. 249)

What Freud leaves out of this consideration of loss and mourning is the shame and humiliation of not being able to connect with others, of being alone without any adequate means of expressing one's isolation, with no one to express it to, since one has brought it on oneself.

12. Sam commented,

When I was sick I was thinking about Sartre's book *Nausea*. All you see around you is minuscule detail: a tap dripping. You're locked into this. All you can think of is this incredible detail of the tap dripping in the moment, nothing more, nothing less. Day after day, it's always the same. The same tap dripping. . . . At the end of our sessions I try to anticipate, to switch off before you say we have to stop. At the slightest hint I'm not wanted, I disconnect, and can't keep hold.

13. Freud writes in *Mourning and Melancholia*, "This substitution of identification for object-love is an important mechanism in the narcissistic afflictions" (1917, p. 249). Again what Freud misses has much to do with the effects of the defense mechanisms he has so brilliantly characterized. In this case, he stops short of identifying the shame entailed in not being able to establish object relations, a shame experienced as yet another Oedipal defeat.

14. The entire situation recalls the passage of Kierkegaard in *Sickness Unto Death* in which he speaks of the dilemma of the despairer (one who is ashamed). It is

> as if a writer were to make a slip of the pen, and the error became conscious of itself as such—perhaps it wasn't a mistake but from a much higher point of view an essential ingredient in the whole presentation—and as if this error now wanted to rebel against the author, out of hatred for him forbid him to correct it, and in manic defiance say to him: "No, I will not be erased, I will stand as a witness against you, a witness to the fact that you are a second-rate author." (1849, p. 105)

Such an attitude of hateful resentment toward attempts at correction indicate difficulties with our ideals of who we feel we (and others) ought to be.

15. Fenichel (1945, p. 139).

16. Sartre defines shame as

> the consciousness of being irremediably what I always was: "in suspense"—that is, in the mode of the not-yet or of the "already-no-longer." Pure shame is not a feeling of being this or that guilty object but in general of being an object, that is, of recognizing myself in this degraded, fixed and dependent being which I am for the Other. Shame is the feeling of an original fall, not because of the fact that I may have committed this or that particular fault, but simply that I have "fallen" into the world in the midst of things and that I need the mediation of the Other in order to be what I am. (1964, p. 264)

17. Pirandello (1994, p. 51).

18. "His mother having died so suddenly, Silvio had felt another darkness gathering in his soul in addition to that of his blindness: another, much more terrible darkness, in the face of which all men are blind. But people with good eyes can at least find distraction from that other darkness by looking at the things around them; he could not. Blind in life, he was now blind in death as well. And into this other darkness, more bare, more cold, more shadowy, his mother had disappeared, silently, leaving him behind alone, in a frightening void." Ibid., p. 55.

19. Ibid., p. 57.

20. Ibid., p. 73.

CHAPTER THREE

1. See, for example, Peristiany (1965).

2. Spiro (1987) has developed the concept of culturally constituted defense mechanisms, a notion I have also taken up (Kilborne, 1981c). The anthropological tradition of interest in culture and defense mechanisms can be associated with the school of Culture and Personality that flourished particularly after World War II. See also Devereux (1972, 1976a, 1980).

3. In chapter six we will take up Renoir's variations on this theme.

4. See Machiavelli, *The Prince* and *The Discourses* as well as his *Discourses on Livy*. One of the most cogent recent essays on this subject is that of Nagel, "The Shredding of Public Privacy: Reflections on Recent Events in Washington" (1998).

5. Pirandello, *The Late Mattia Pascal* (1964, p. 145).

6. Ibid., p. 146.

7. Williams (1993, p. 78).

8. Ibid., p. 73.

9. Ibid., pp. 78–79.

10. Bentley (1952, p. xviii).

11. "Tuzza and all Agrigento looking on; the Ponza-Frola trio and the whole provincial capital looking on; Henry IV—a spectacle for his friends and his servants; the six characters—a drama to amaze actors and stage manager; Delia Morello—with her double out front and actors on stage discussing the author; Mommina—dying in a play within a play" (Ibid., pp. xviii–xix).

12. As Laudisi explains,

Now Madame, I beg of you do not tell your husband, nor my sister, nor my niece, nor Signor Cinia here, what you think of me; because if you were to do that, they would all tell you you are completely wrong. But, you see, you are really right; because I am really what you take me to be; though, my dear madam, that does not prevent me from also being really what your husband, my sister, my niece, and Signora Cinia take me to be— because they are also absolutely right. (Pirandello, 1952, p. 7)

13. "Those people have concealed those documents in themselves, in their own souls. Can't you understand that? She has created for him, or he for her, a world of fancy which has all the earmarks of reality itself. And in that fictitious world they get along perfectly well and in full accord with each other" (p. 98).

14. Speaking of the difficulty of establishing truth even within one person, as Josephs notes, "there are a number of conflicting views to be had atop the iceberg" that depend upon "conflicting modes of self-observation, self-reflection, and self-analysis, both conscious and unconscious" (1997, p. 427).

15. In the story version, Pirandello notes that each character has the most exquisite consideration for the madness of the other; both are so rational that were it not for their allegations of madness, the townsfolk would never have suspected anything was wrong.

16. Pirandello (1933, p. 183).

17. *Los Angeles Times*, November 1, 1997.

18. For Pirandello, who blurs and scrambles the lines between comedy and tragedy, theater is at bottom "a farce which in presenting a tragedy included its self-parody and self-caricature, but not as superimposed elements; instead they were like the projections of shadows from its own body, awkward shadows that accompanied every tragic gesture" (1933, p. 22).

19. Referring to the modern Italian theater of the grotesque as transcendental farce, Pirandello explains this with reference to Hegelian philosophy. And in *One* . . . there is a note preceding the text that stands for Pirandello's vision of tragedy. "This book not only depicts dramatically, but at the same time demonstrates by what might be termed a mathematical method, the impossibility of any human creature's being to others what he is to himself." For a further elaboration of these themes as they are taken up by Renoir, see chapter 7.

20. Pirandello, Humor (p. 17).

21. Similarly, in "A Passing Touch" the protagonist, an aging but robust and womanizing German living in Rome since early childhood, unexpectedly suffers a stroke. As a result, and with no consciousness whatsoever of what he is doing, he forgets his Italian and reverts to German. At a park with a friend who has also had a stroke, the two partially paralyzed, aging men exercise in machines, where they are seen by a former girlfriend who treats them like the children they have become, kissing them on the brow and feeding them biscuits. All that is needed is "a passing touch" and we become—or are revealed to be (which comes to the same thing)—someone else, someone who speaks another language, reduced from a vital being to a pathetic, ridiculous, helpless figure.

CHAPTER FOUR

1. In his astonishing paper, "On Screen Memories" Freud (1899) suggests that one memory can hide another, an unconscious process by which what we do not want to see and know is protected by other, less threatening, memories.

2. Schneider (1977, p. 35).

3. Four men were gathered together in a major Hollywood studio with a single woman, who mentioned "the most basic human fear." When asked what that was, she replied, "the fear of being invisible."

4. See Rosenbaum (1994, pp. 29ff.).

5. *New York Times*, April 30, 1995.

6. Sheldon (1994, p. 6).

7. Ibid., pp. 321–322.

8. Ibid., p. 58.

9. Ibid., p. 61.

10. See Winnicott (1958).

11. Sheldon (1994, pp. 172–173). This is a reference to the period during which Potter was working on the Puddle Duck series.

12. Quoted in ibid., p. 289.

13. Ibid., p. 176.

14. Recent (1999) interviews with Victor Cherakshin, former number 2 man in Washington and handler of Aldrich Ames, point up the mirror shows of the cold war. The FBI exaggerated what Ames told the Soviets, Cherakshin explains, in order to make themselves look as though they were in control. Had Kryuchov and the KGB moved more slowly against the moles—taking several years to feed them disinformation—the CIA might never have discovered it had been betrayed.

15. Ellison (1990, p. 509).

16. Ibid., p. 579.

17. Ibid., p. 573.

18. Kafka (1971, p. 272).

19. Ibid., p. 276.

20. Ibid., p. 277.

21. Pirandello (1926, pp. 25ff.).

22. Ibid., pp. 114–116.

23. *New Yorker*, February 28, 1994 (p. 76).

24. Nagel (1998) has also written of performing musicians and has similarly found that physical pain (e.g., in bowing arms or in the hands or wrists of pianists) can have both psychological consequences and psychological causes.

25. Gabbard (1977, 1979, 1983) has written of the performer's fear of exposure and the pain this entails, associating this with the feeling of being naked and transparent. The "emotional incontinence" (Nagel, 1998) of professional musicians and performers expresses the fear of not being able to exhibit sufficient mastery, of having something untoward hang out.

26. Hegel says something similar when, in speaking of Force, an admittedly woolly concept, he notes, "Force, taken as that in which [constitutive elements] have disappeared, is Force *proper*" (1807, p. 81). The process of disappearing (and of negation) transforms becoming into being for itself, and as such constitutes the only truth to which human beings can ever be privy. Force "has really the significance of sheer vanishing" (p. 85). To disappear from the confusing world of sense perceptions can for Hegel, as for Plato, mean being born into the untainted world of conceptual truths. Throughout Hegel there are implications of dying and being born again into another world. The "suprasensible" is attained only by a kind of blindness or dying in the "sensible" world. And later on he concludes the section on "Force and the Understanding." "For this knowledge of what is the truth of appearance as ordinarily conceived, and of its inner being, is itself only a result of a complex movement whereby the modes of consciousness 'meaning', perceiving, and the Understanding vanish . . ." (p. 103).

27. *New York Review of Books*, September 27, 1990.

CHAPTER FIVE

1. Pirandello (1931, p. 67).

2. Ibid., pp. 90–94.

3. Ibid., p. 112.

4. Ibid., p. 216. And she adds later that she cannot recognize herself even in her diaries, "in which she had set down new words on the day of the wedding: 'They say, you know, that now he will have to *see* you.' That notebook is mine, and I am taking it with me! And I have all the more reason to do so since, strangely enough, the writing appears to be in my hand!" (p. 219).

5. Susan was ashamed of me for not seeing her, ashamed of her wish to look, enraged at me for not already having seen, enraged at herself for needing me to see, and so forth.

6. Freud (1920, p. 14).

7. Ibid., p. 15.

8. But if this is so, then what are we to make of Freud's point that the game represents a cultural achievement (renunciation)? What is the child renouncing in the way of instinctual satisfaction if he is helpless anyway? And where is the pleasure (the reduction of tension) either in such renunciation, or, if the game is an expression of being abandoned, in the reversal of the situation such that it is the *child* who abandons the object that symbolizes his mother?

9. Generally speaking, those writing on peek-a-boo have followed Freud's lead in emphasizing mastery rather than shame, rage, and Oedipal defeat. Federn (1952) held that peek-a-boo, dropping and retrieving objects, constituted part of normal development which, when not vigorous and pleasurable, indicates ill-health and frailty in ego development. Similarly, Spitz (1957) emphasized the functions of peekaboo in identification, just as he stressed the predominance of identification as a psychological process in the second year of life. Erikson (1950) discusses holding on and letting go, as two modalities in identification and ego development, following the same general lines as other writers on the subject. Winnicott (1958), with his usual flair for clear, creative formulations, dates the game of throwing things (peekaboo?) to between seven and nine months, associating it with readiness to wean, a more concrete way of saying that the "games" (if we can call them that) represent attempts at separation. No doubt the loss of the breast can trigger shame reactions and rage at not being able to control what one needs. For Winnicott, peekaboo defines "transitional space," originating "in the same developmental period as transitional object formation; it is a bridge between an autocratic activity and an expression of true object relations" (1953, p. 267).

10. Susan had to make *herself* disappear rather than play with the "lost" object, whether her mother, her toys, her teddies, her analyst, or any transitional object. And there was in her play no "reappearance. When Freud discusses disappearance also, he does so in the context of mastery, not of shame and Oedipal defeat. Freud continues:

> One day the child's mother had been away for several hours and on her return was met with the words "Baby-o-o-o-o-o-!" which was at first incomprehensible. It soon turned out, however, that during this long period of solitude the child had found a method

of making *himself* disappear. He had discovered his reflection in a full-length mirror which did not quite reach to the ground, so that by crouching down he could make his mirror image "gone." (1920, p. 15)

"Gone" is only play if "not gone" or retrieval (not lost) is possible; otherwise, gone is ominous, fateful, serious, and all too real. In this case the very possibility of play would seem to depend on healthy object relations. Also, in this text Freud refers to a narcissistic wound. "Loss of love and failure leave behind them a permanent injury to self-regard in the form of a narcissistic scar" (p. 20).

11. In his paper on eye symbolism Ferenczi (1913) mentions several similar patients: one whose myopia contributed to a keen sense of shame, attributable in his mind to his shortsightedness, which Ferenczi relates to sadomasochism; and a second patient who at puberty developed a dread of seeing himself in the mirror. While Ferenczi related these dynamics to displacement from genitalia, I do not think it is necessary to do so in order to appreciate their dynamics. Indeed, sometimes focusing on the sexual meanings of, for example, nearsightedness, can provide a cover of guilt that keeps the shame dynamics unavailable to the analysis and allows both analyst and analysand to shy away from the pain of the experience being described. It was, I think, important for Susan to express fully just how unbearable she felt the pain of not being able to see herself "with a face" to be.

12. Freud quotes Keller's allusion to Homer's *Odyssey* in *The Interpretation of Dreams* (1900–1901, p. 246). Susan's sense of being "caught between two worlds," is reminiscent of the theme of doubleness, seeing double and double-mapping in nineteenth- and twentieth-century literature, of what Arnold described in the 1850s as "Wandering between two worlds, one dead / The other powerless to be born."

13. Krausz (1994, pp. 59–72).

14. Krausz suggests that Freud placed too much emphasis on verbal memories, and neglected the power of the visual, even though he recognized that visual thinking, being closer to the unconscious, occurs earlier in development than does symbolic thinking. Krausz believes her patient used the discrepancy between visual and verbal memory defensively. Krausz's patient "hid her developing private self in a visual world, which allowed her to remain 'invisible' in the verbal world she had to share with others" (p. 63).

15. Quindlen (1994).

16. *New York Review of Books* (September 21, 1995).

An old revolutionary utopia, whether fascist or communist: life without secrets, where public life and private life are one and the same. The surrealist dream André Breton loved: the glass house, a house without curtains where man lives in full view of the world. Ah, the beauty of transparency. The only successful realization of this dream: a society totally monitored by the public. . . .

When I arrived in France from that Czechoslovakia bristling with microphones, I saw on a magazine cover a large photo of Jacques Brel hiding his face from photographers who had tracked him down in front of the hospital where he was being treated for his already advanced cancer. And, suddenly, I felt I was encountering the very same evil that had made me flee my country; broadcasting Prochazka's conversations and photographing a dying singer hiding his face seemed to belong to the same world: I said to myself that when it becomes the custom and the rule to divulge another person's private life, we are entering a time when the highest stake is the survival or disappearance of the individual.

CHAPTER SIX

1. Bergan (1955, p. 203).

2. "Il est capable de traverser l'Atlantique, mais n'est pas foutu de traverser les Champs Elysées hors des clous."

3. See Kris (1982) for an overview of the subject.

4. Menand (*New York Review of Books*, March 23, 1995).

5. Similarly, analysts seek to approach each patient "unboxed by moral resolution."

6. Bergan (1955, p. 205).

7. Renoir was no doubt familiar with all the various meanings of the bear in European lore. No doubt he knew well the splendid Chekov play, *The Bear*. Also, as Adamson (1997) points out, in Melville, bear imagery is invariably associated with gloom, misanthropy, and solitude.

8. Pirandello (1926, p. 262).

9. Pirandello (1988, p. xxi), Introduction to *Six Characters in Search of an Author*.

10. You will recall the passage quoted earlier. The Father explains, "It won't be me, as I feel myself to be inside here." A sentiment echoed by the Producer, who admonishes the Father. "There is no place here for you, as yourself. Here you just don't exist. An actor represents you, that's it" (Ibid., 1988, p. 36).

11. Bergan (1955, pp. 351–352).

12. Ibid., p. 314.

13. Ibid., p. 317.

14. Quoted in Adamson (1997, p. 15).

CHAPTER SEVEN

1. Simon (1988, p. 1).

2. See Kilborne (1992b) on the role of faith in the social sciences for an analysis of the ways in which Durkheim's emphasis on social solidarity and collective representations strikes root in the French Revolution and in the positivism of Comte. The religious sociology that Durkheim had in mind is one that provides a response to "anomie," and is therefore a social antidote to boredom and inaction.

3. There has been some interest in Adam and Eve over the past couple of decades. The most prominent book in the literature is Pagles's *Adam, Eve and the Serpent* (1988). But a number of writers, particularly seventeenth-century specialists, have made notable contributions (e.g., Popkin, Katz, and Mandlebaum).

4. See, for example, the entry on "sin" written by LeCocque in the *Encyclopedia of Religion* (1987).

5. Broucek begins his book with a brief discussion of the Genesis myth, writing that the world as we know it begins with shame. While he suggests the importance of the myth in representing to us distinctions between inside and outside, he limits his discussion to the register of mastery rather than that of humiliation. "As something now external, opaque, and heavy, the world had to be probed, seen through, and weighed; as unintelligible it had to be studied and researched; as hostile, it had to be subdued and controlled or destroyed" (1991, p. 4).

6. Ricoeur (1967, pp. 70ff.).

7. Lewis, quoted in Adamson (1997).

8. Milton, *Paradise Lost* (1640–1665, iv: 73–75).

9. Ibid., iv: 193–195.

10. Ibid., iv: 396–399.

11. Ibid., iv: 505–508.

12. Ibid., iv: 801ff.

13. Ibid., iv: 312–320.

14. Earlier versions of portions of the next two sections appeared under the title "The Missing Self that Goes Unnoticed" in Adamson and Clark, *Scenes of Shame: Psychoanalysis, Shame, and Writing* (1999).

15. Kierkegaard (1855, p. 61).

16. "In the state of innocence man is not merely an animal, for if at any time of his life he was merely an animal, he never would become a man. So then the spirit is present, but is in a state of dreaming" (p. 39).

17. During his own lifetime Kierkegaard's idea of "the individual" drew much attention ("bitter notoriety"). It provided a model for Ibsen's moralizing and cocksure Dr. Stockmann in "An Enemy of the People." In his emphasis on the individual, Kierkegaard draws upon the tradition of Augustine and Luther. Kierkegaard takes up the Thomistic notion that man is a finite, body-soul complex, but he revises his definition to include man as a creature of passions. For Kierkegaard the will is a major natural passion. Kierkegaard's notion of the individual's relation to God, his dialectic of "Thou and I," was later to be taken up by Buber, Berdyaev, and by other personalists, and, more recently, by interpersonalists. In treating the other as "thou" one responds to him or her with all that is most intimate and personal (Collins, 1983, p. 199), a position pertinent for notions of transference, particularly in the light of Kierkegaard's emphasis on man as a creature of passions.

18. My emphasis here is different from most commentators on Kierkegaard, who tend to stress guilt and to ignore shame.

19. As Wurmser (1981) has pointed out, shame has everything to do with dialectical processes. Hegel writes, "And experience is the name we give to just this movement, in which the immediate, the inexperienced . . . becomes alienated from itself and then returns to itself from this alienation . . ." (1807, p. 21).

20. It is worth pausing for a moment to further consider Kierkegaard's critique of Hegel. Kierkegaard held that the Hegelians would in fact like to assume a role with respect to human history given only to God (Collins, 1983, pp. 135–136).

Kierkegaard criticizes Hegelian philosophy for threatening the personal individual-God bond. It "suffers from the perspectival illusion of viewing history as the freedom of necessity," simply because it is already and cannot be changed" (p. 136). In Kierkegaard's eyes, Hegel went wrong when, in reaction to Kant, he essentially equated thought and being (p. 124).

Characterizing Kierkegaard's critiques of Hegel, Collins notes (a) that Hegel does not understand that existence "can never be subsumed within a system of finite thought, no matter how broad and inclusive its principles and method"; (b) that Hegel is inept in dealing metaphysically with the basic notions of being and becoming because of "his failure to distinguish between these concepts in their logical status and as representative of objects, which are themselves nonconceptual"; and (c) that Hegel's theory of world history is "inimical to man's ethical life as a responsible individual" (pp. 119–120).

21. For Kierkegaard, the self is "a relation which relates to itself. . . . The self is not the relation but the relation's relating to itself" (1849, p. 43).

22. "A logical system is possible; an existential system is impossible" (1855, p. 121).

23. Collins (1983, p. 174).

24. For Kierkegaard, Hegel cannot account for change despite his notion of negation and dialectic because he views the negative as evil, a criticism that draws upon Kierkegaard's background in theology, in which evil is more and other than negation. See also Ricoeur (1967).

25. Since Kohut and the Self-Psychologists, the concept of a self-disorder has come into the psychoanalytic/psychotherapeutic vocabulary. But there is to my knowledge no mention of Kierkegaard in the writings of Kohut or the Self-Psychologists.

26. "This self, which should have been her richesse—though in another sense just as much in despair—has become, now that 'he' is dead, a loathsome void. . . . To despair over oneself, in despair to want to be rid of oneself is the formula for all despair" (Kierkegaard, 1849, p. 50).

27. Ibid., p. 43.

28. Ibid., p. 57.

29. Ibid.

30. The Greeks, notes Hegel, thought of the void as the principle of motion, although they did not go so far as to identify the negative as the self. Hegel writes,

The disparity which exists in consciousness between the "I" and the substance which is its object is the distinction between them, the *negative* in general. This can be regarded as the *defect* of both, though it is their soul, or that which moves them. That is why some of the ancients conceived the void as the principle of motion, for they rightly saw the moving principle as the negative, though they did not as yet grasp that the negative is the self. Now, although this negative appears at first as a disparity between the "I" and its object, it is just as much the disparity of the substance with itself. Thus what seems to happen outside of it, to be an activity directed against it, is really its own doing, and Substance shows itself to be essentially Subject. (1807, p. 21)

31. Kierkegaard (1849, pp. 66–67).

32. Ibid., p. 67.

33. As Kierkegaard observes in *The Concept of Dread* (1855, p. 46), "What it [the self] understands itself to be is in the final instance a riddle; just when it seems on the point of having the building finished, at a whim it can dissolve the whole thing into nothing."

34. Kierkegaard (1849, p. 101).

35. Pirandello (1964, p. 83).

36. Ibid., p. 85.

37. Ibid., p. 121.

38. Ibid., p. 189.

39. Ibid., p. 221.

40. Kierkegaard (1849, p. 147).

41. Ibid., p. 62.

CHAPTER EIGHT

1. The psychoanalytic literature on the superego and the ego ideal is enormous and fascinating. Freud developed the notions (e.g, 1914a, 1915a, 1917, 1920, 1921, 1923, 1926) summarized by Rappaport (1957). Recently they have been taken up and elaborated in asssociation with shame by, for example, Wurmser (1981, 1987, 1997); Lansky and Morrison (1997); and Morrison (1989, 1996). Others (e.g., Blos, 1974 and Chasseguet-Smirgel, 1974, 1976, 1985) have written on the subject, although not explicitly with shame in mind. I hope it will be clear that this book also depends heavily on the concepts of superego and ego ideal to describe shame dynamics.

2. There are a number of legends and tales that also contain the prohibition against looking, such as the tale of Melusine, in which Melusine,

the daughter of a fairy, marries Raymondin on the condition that he never look at her on Saturdays. Eventually, Raymondin breaks down and looks. Melusine turns into a snake and vanishes forever.

3. What makes the look lethal? How can looks maim? Bonnet suggests that the exhibitionist attempts to see his genitals by looking at his image in the look of the other. By implication, if he fails in his attempts to "discover himself" in the looks of others, he will feel increasingly intense shame, hatred and, particularly, rage (1996, p. 13).

4. Bonnet writes, "C'est le regard que lui renvoie le reflet qu'il a en face de lui." (p. 19) "Ce qui tue Narcisse, c'est d'avoir regardé le soleil en face, d'avoir voulu regarder le regard" (p. 20). "It is the look that reflects back to him what he is confronted with. What kills Narcissus is to have looked at the sun straight on, to have wanted to see the look." [my translation]

5. See ibid., p. 55. To see what one reveals of oneself, in fantasy one must appropriate the eye of the other, the mythical eye (p. 145), "an eye for an eye."

6. The role of fantasy in shame dynamics cannot be underestimated. See, for example, Rizzuto (1991) and Kilborne (1999b), and on psychic reality and unconscious belief, for example, Britton (1995).

7. It is not enough just to take the other's eye, one must make the eye that sees disappear. "To see, one must kill" (Bonnet, 1996, p. 258).

8. Mahoney (1989). Freud introduced the notion of a drive to look at (Schaulust) in the *Three Essays on Sexuality* (1905) and took it up subsequently in, for example, his 1920 paper, "Psychogenic Disturbance of Vision" and in the opening section from his *Metaphychology* (1914). Patrick Mahoney has been of real help to me in exploring the role of vision in Freud's writings and in urging me to read a number of French authors with whom I was unfamliar (e.g., Bonnet, 1996).

9. See the entries on "narcissism" in Laplanche and Pontalis, *Vocabulaire de la psychanalyse.*

10. Freud (1914a, p. 94).

11. Ibid., p. 95.

12. Particularly after 1913, Freud tended to link scopophilia, exhibitionism, and shame, but never brought them into focus dynamically and affectively. He tended to see them as defenses against aggressive and libidinal drives, rather than essential for self-consciousness.

13. What Freud appears to be referring to in *Mourning and Melancholia* (1917) is identification in which the object is experienced to regulate self-esteem.

14. Ibid., p. 246.

15. Ibid., p. 249.

16. "This substitution of identification for object love is an important mechanism in the narcissistic afflictions. . . . It represents, of course, a *regression* from one type of object-choice, that it is the first way—and one that is expressed in an ambivalent fashion—in which the ego picks out an object. The ego wants to incorporate this object into itself, and, in accordance with the oral or cannibalistic phase of libidinal development in which it is, it wants to do so by devouring it. Abraham is undoubtedly right in attributing to this connection the refusal of nourishment met with in severe forms of melancholia." (pp. 249–250)

17. In "The mirror stage as formative of the function of the I as revealed in psychoanalytic experience" [Le Stade du Miroir] (*Ecrits*, 1966), the address delivered at the Sixteenth International Congress of Psychoanalysis, Zurich, 1949, Lacan addresses the "mirror stage" of development, characterizing it as "an identification," "the threshold of the visible world," which entails a shift from "the specular I" to the "social I." But, as I read Lacan, the hypothesis that there ever can be such a "missing link" between the "specular I" and the "social I" misses the more important point about shame dynamics, namely that they defy inside/outside dichotomies. For me, however suggestive Lacan's ideas may be, they always remain just out of reach. Implicit in this paper, and the others, is an attack on Loewenstein, his analyst, and a major figure in ego psychology. Why Loewenstein had the influence he did on psychoanalysis in France is a fascinating question, related in part perhaps to the fact that he was Marie Bonaparte's lover (Roudinesco, 1986, p. 118). It is a fact that Loewenstein opposed the membership of Lacan into the French Psychoanalytic Society, and that the antagonism between the two profoundly influenced Lacan's thinking.

18. Compare the mirror transference of Kohut, together with the mirroring selfobject (see Kohut, 1971, 1984).

19. Grunberger (1979) can therefore focus on narcissistic regression as a fantasized return to a "real" state, an anchor in biological experience. Grunberger and those who take a similar position do not ascribe importance to the dynamics of looking in their ideas of narcissism.

20. An economic description of such wounding in terms of investments of psychic energy leads to the use of the term *narcissism*; an affective

description leads to the use of the term *shame*. One of the confusing features of Self-Psychology is the confounding of these two levels of description. Freud himself has something to say about shame when he speaks of narcissism. And, generally speaking, the *affects* of shame are only very rarely rigorously distinguished from the metapsychological *theories* of narcissism.

21. Melville, *Moby Dick* (1988, p. 543).

22. "The Curse of Self-esteem," *Newsweek*, February 17, 1992.

23. Hollander (1975, p. 393).

24. Ibid., p. 394. See Hollander's *Seeing Through Clothes* (1975) and J. P. Vernant (e.g., 1985) for discussions of mirror iconography. René Magritte's painting *Reproduction Interdite* expresses the idea that any mirror can show no more than is actually visible.

25. Ibid., pp. 395–396.

26. See Anzieu, *L'auto-analyse de Freud*.

27. Freud (1900–1901, p. 421).

28. Ibid., p. 422.

29. Ibid. Writing of punishment dreams, Freud compares the dreams of a parvenu to the dreams of a journeyman tailor who had grown into a famous author. But how does it become possible for a dream, in the conflict between a parvenu's pride and his self-criticism, to side with the latter, and choose as its content a sensible warning instead of an unlawful wish fulfillment? (pp. 475ff.).

30. Ibid., p. 121.

31. Wurmser (1981, p. 306).

32. Freud (1900–1901, vol. 4, pp. 452ff.).

33. Ibid., pp. 477–478

34. Ibid., pp. 242ff.

35. Ibid., pp. 248ff.

36. Ibid., p. 317.

37. Ibid., p.318.

38. Ibid., p. 245.

39. Ibid., p. 243.

40. As Pirandello notes, "You can only know yourself when you strike an attitude: a statue: not alive. When one is alive, one lives and does not see

himself. To know one's self is to die . . . however much you may try, you can never know yourself as others see you. And of what use is it, then, to know one's self for one's self's sake?" (1933, pp. 247–249).

41. *New Yorker*, October 1997 (pp. 68ff.).

42. See, for example, Poland (1992).

43. See, for example, Golberger (1995). And on safety and danger in the analytic situation, see Levy and Inderbitzin (1997).

44. See Silber's (1976) review of Allen's book *The Fear of Looking or Scopophilic-exhibitionistic Conflicts* (1974). I have come to think that in many cases the necessary regression in analytic work cannot be brought about without dealing with appearances, Oedipal shame, with looking and being looked at in the transference.

45. Expressing the vain need to rely upon appearances for pride and love, one of Pirandello's characters ponders the question of identity. "Ah, if each of us were able to detach ourselves for a moment from that metaphor of ourselves that we are inevitably impelled to form from our innumerable conscious and unconscious pretenses and the fictional interpretations of our acts and sentiments, it would be immediately clear that this *him* is *another*, another who has nothing or little to do with him, and that the true *him* is the one who is screaming within, his guilt, the intimate being often condemned for a whole life to remain unknown to us! We wish at all costs to save, to keep upright that metaphor of ourselves that is our pride and our love. And for this metaphor we suffer martyrdom." *The Notebooks of Serafino Gubbio* (quoted on p. 91 in Caputi, 1991).

46. "On the other hand I do feel the pleasure-gratification of the attacker, which I am still able to perceive. The fundamental thesis of all psychology, that the sole function of the psyche is to reduce pain, is therefore preserved. The pain-alleviating function must, however, be able to apply itself not only to one's own ego but also to every kind of pain perceived or imagined by the psyche" (Ferenczi, 1988, p. 104).

CHAPTER NINE

1. Westermarck (1901, 1926).

2. Speaking of defenses against sexual instincts, Freud details four kinds: reversal (active to passive, or reversal of content), turning against the self, repression, and sublimation. "The active aim (to torture, to look at) is replaced by the passive aim (to be tortured, to be looked at). Reversal of content is found in the single instance of the transformation of love into hate" (Freud, 1915a, p. 127).

3. Ibid., p. 129.

4. At the end of this text, Freud summarizes.

We may sum up by saying that the essential feature in the vicis-situdes undergone by instincts lies in *the subjection of the instinctual impulses to the influences of the three great polarities that dominate mental life.* Of these three polarities we might describe that of activity—passivity as the *biological,* that of ego—external world as the *real,* and finally that of pleasure—unpleasure as the *economic* polarity. (p. 140)

5. Bergler (p. 66).

6. See, for example, Hargreaves-Mawdsley (1963).

7. Carlyle, *Sartor Resartus* (1908, p. 52).

8. Ibid.

9. Van der Velde (1985) and others emphasize that it is in the nature of our visual perception to be limited in such a way we cannot perceive our body as a whole, a point made also by Snell (1953) in his work on the ancient Greeks.

10. Given the importance of the subject and its prevalence throughout the Mediterranean, it is surprising there is not more written on the subject. What there is (e.g., Peristiany, 1965) seldom combines clinical experience with an exploration of the subject. Also, the literature is mostly in Italian.

11. See Mellinkoff's (1993) discussion of the dishonor associated with patterned colors (e.g., Deirick Bouts, Jorg Breu, and Johann Koerbecke) (p. 24). Certain groups (i.e., foot soldiers and executioners) continued to wear patterned costume long after it was outmoded in other parts of society. These were fixed in the sixteenth century and continued into the nineteenth (p. 27).

12. Siebert (1996).

13. Bearing in mind my discussion of modesty, shame, and nakedness in the story of Adam and Eve, consider these lines of Sartre:

Modesty and in particular the fear of being surprised in a state of nakedness are only a symbolic specification of original shame; the body symbolizes our defenseless state as objects. To put on clothes is to hide one's object state; it is to claim the right of see-ing without being seen; that is, to be pure subject. This is why the Biblical symbol of the fall after the original sin is the fact that Adam and Eve "know they are naked." (1964, p. 265)

14. My discussion of Clothe the Naked owes much to a previous paper using the play (Kilborne, 1995a).

15. "Perhaps," comments Ludovico, " you saw yourself in some fabulous apartment," since this is what he would have done in her place. But Ersilia replies, "Oh no, I didn't see myself anywhere" (1988, p. 142). Then, almost immediately, Ersilia breaks off to say how ashamed she is, since she does not feel she deserves the good fortune.

16. Ibid., p. 143.

17. Ibid., p. 143.

18. Ibid., p. 144. Such questions are not in the imaginary script Ludovico is inventing, so, irritated, he asks, "Why do you want to know?" To which Ersilia replies: "Because I would like to be just like the girl you imagined." Still unable to believe Ludovico could genuinely be interested in her, Ersilia warily inquires further. "But if what interested you, reading that paper, was the story of that other girl, if it was *she* who captured your imagination, then *I* . . . (She stops, rather lost)." And later on, mistrustfully, "If *she's* not *me*, then you don't believe my story" (p. 145).

19. Ibid., p. 146.

20. Ersilia attempts to explain herself to Ludovico. "Please at least— at least let me be her. . . . The girl you imagined in my story. If only I could— might be—someone of importance, just once, as you said. Let me be the girl you imagined. *Me* as I am, like this." But then Ersilia nails her predicament by adding, "Somehow you seem to betray me always by seeing *her* instead of me. . . . I was the one who didn't want to go on living. The one who suffered all the misfortunes. I think I have the right to be the girl in the novel you will write" (p. 152).

21. As she says to Ludovico and Franco, a former lover, "Look, you want to condemn me to be the girl I tried to kill forever? Or will you let her alone, she, and the reason she tried to kill herself. *She* was Ersilia, but what she said doesn't count any more, neither for you nor for me" (p. 175). Ersilia finds she cannot see herself in Franco, cannot feel any viable bond between them.

22. When Ersilia says she wants to go away it is clear she has no idea where. "Disappear—just get swallowed up down there in the street! I don't know! (p. 167).

23. Ibid., p. 176.

24. Having accused the others of living in a world of falsehood and fictions, Ersilia cries out, "No, this is real life. This is what I tried to get

rid of, but it refuses to let me go (She becomes hysterical). It's sunk its teeth into me and it won't let me go; How can I get away? Where can I go?" (p. 177).

25. Ibid., pp. 206–207.

26. Rushdie goes on, "Our lives teach us who we are. I have learned the hard way that when you permit anyone else's description of reality to supplant your own—and such descriptions have been raining down on me, from security advisers, governments, journalists, Archbishops, friends, enemies, mullahs—then you might as well be dead." *New York Times Book Review*, 1996.

27. Matthew Green (1696–1737), English poet and author of a poem entitled *The Spleen*, writes,

> Somtimes I dress, with women sit,
> And chat away the gloomy fit;
> Quit the stiff garb of serious sense
> And wear a gay impertinence. . . .
> Talk of unusual swell of waist
> In maid of honour loosely laced,
> And beauty borrowing Spanish red,
> And loving pair with separate bed,
> And jewels pawned for loss of game,
> And then redeemed by loss of fame. . . .
> And thus in modish manner we
> In aid of sugar, sweeten tea.

CHAPTER TEN

1. Freud comments that just as Kant (e.g., *Critique of Pure Reason*, 1881) warned us

> not to overlook the fact that our perceptions are subjectively conditioned and must not be regarded as identical with what is perceived though unknowable, so psycho-analysis warns us not to equate perceptions by means of consciousness with the unconscious mental processes which are their object. Like the physical, the psychical is not necessarily in reality what it appears to us to be. We shall be glad to learn, however, that the correction of internal perception will turn out not to offer such great difficulties as the correction of external perception—that internal objects are less unknowable than the external world. (1915b, p. 171)

2. As Sartre notes, *"Through shame we confer on the Other an indubitable presence."* [my italics] He continues, "the Other does not constitute me as an object for myself but for him . . ." (1964, p. 251). Then Sartre uses the following example. When I hear footsteps behind me and feel alarmed, what I am responding to is not my conscious thought that there is someone there who may be dangerous, but rather my perception that I feel vulnerable, that I am seen by someone I cannot "see" in the widest sense, which includes whatever I might imagine. Sartre continues, speaking of the shame "that I have a body which can be hurt, that I occupy a place and that I cannot in any case escape from the space in which I am without defense—in short, that I am seen" (p. 235). Being seen creates the other as "an internal hemorrhage," a sort of "drain hole" (p. 233).

3. The character in Hawthorne's *The Scarlet Letter* (1850). See Dolis (1993) and Adamson (1999), whose study of shame in *The Scarlet Letter* is particularly probing and thorough. Kilborne (2001) suggests that the shame of the Reverend Dimmesdale is both less visible and more pernicious than that of Hester Prynne, who can wear her shame publically, as a badge. Both are rooted in unconscious conflicts, but Dimmesdale's is less bearable because less representable than Hester's, a point driven home by Hawthorne's deliberately ambiguous description of Dimmesdale's end.

4. This section reworks material appearing in Kilborne (1998a).

5. Ferenczi, *The Clinical Diaries* (1985, p. 62).

6. Ferenczi (1985) pursued this critique of Freud in the diary entry of May 1, 1932 ["Who is crazy, we or the patients? (the children or the adults?)"] when he writes, "Since making this discovery [that hysterics lie] Freud no longer loves his patients. He has returned to the love of his well-ordered and cultivated superego (a further proof of this being his antipathy toward and deprecating remarks about psychotics, perverts, and everything in general that is "too abnormal"). And then Ferenczi delivers his blow. "[Freud's] therapeutic method, like his theory, is becoming more and more [influenced] by his interest in order, character, the replacement of a bad superego by a better one; he is becoming pedagogical" (p. 93). Not finding Freud willing or ready to admit to failings, Ferenczi, sensitive to shame and narcissistic wounding, writes of the need for the analyst to admit to failings.

7. Quoted in Bonomi (1999).

8. See Bonomi's excellent discussion of this episode.

9. Ferenczi's shame and humiliation over his needs for gratification and response from Freud, and over his (Ferenczi's) inability to communicate to Freud the pain he felt in such a way that Freud could understand it, probably contributed to Ferenczi's development of the concept of mutual analysis.

10. Also important is what Ferenczi refers to in the "Confusion of Tongues" paper as "tenderness." See Blum (1994). Because in part of his own personal struggles, Ferenczi focused on understanding the nature of the childhood trauma and humiliation, realized how essential regression is in working such trauma through and, consequently, how important it is for the analyst to recognize whatever in the analytic situation contributes to its repetition rather than its working-through. Ferenczi, particularly, struggled to describe regression (whatever "regression" is construed to mean) experientally, along with the shameful, regressive fears of separation from the analyst, exacerbated by his relationship with Freud.

11. Lasch (1978).

12. See King's *Commissar Vanishes; The Falsification of Photographs and Art in Stalin's Russia* (1997).

13. Quoted in Tolstaya (1998).

14. Ibid.

15. Wurmser, *Mask of Shame* (1981, p. 302).

16. Sartre (1964) writes that we recognize the existence of others because of the uneasiness of shame.

17. Samson Agonistes (lines 73ff.).

18. Lines 561ff. And earlier in the poem the chorus laments,

Which shall I first bewail,
Thy bondage or lost sight,
Prison within prison,
Inseparably dark?
Thou art become (O worst imprisonment!)
The dungeon of thyself; thy soul
(Which men enjoying sight oft without cause complain)
Imprisoned now indeed,
In real darkness of the body dwells,
Shut up from outward light
To incorporate with gloomy night.

(155ff.)

19. Melville wrote of his family, "When there was danger that the family name might be sullied, then the family would close ranks and pretend that nothing unseemly had occurred (quoted in Adamson, 1997, p. 14).

20. Melville, *Moby Dick, or the Whale* (1988, p. 3).

21. Ferenczi writes (1985), "The person splits into a psychic being of pure knowledge that observes the events from the outside, and a totally

insensitive body. Insofar as this psychic being is still accessible to emotions, it turns its interests toward the only feelings left over from the process, that is, the feelings of the attacker" (p. 104).

22. Ferenczi writes, "The withdrawal of love, and being totally alone with one's demands for love against the compact and overwhelming majority, produce shame and repression (neurosis) in so-called normal children." And he continues, "It is as though the psyche, whose sole function it is to reduce emotional tensions and to avoid pain, at the moment of the death of its own person automatically diverts its pain-relieving functions towards the pains, tensions and passions of the attacker, the only person with feelings, that is, identifies with these," ibid.

23. Ibid., p. 163.

24. Pirandello, *The Late Matia Pascal* (1964, p. 47).

25. Ferenczi, *Clinical Diaries* (1985, pp. 32–33).

26. Rangell (1954, p. 6).

27. Quoted in Lanes (1980, pp. 18–19).

28. "That the adults never feel anything similar, that they always and always feel they are right, cleaver and insightful, etc. It is unbearable to be the only bad person in a magnificent and exemplary society, so it is of some consolation when I succeed in making my respected father or teacher lose their tempers, thereby making them admit indirectly that they are not any less subject to 'weakness' than their children" (quoted in Lanes, 1980, p. 167).

29. Marvell (1681).

References

Adamson, Joseph (1997) *Melville, Shame and the Evil Eye; a psychoanalytic reading*. Albany: State University of New York Press.

——— (1999) ed. (with Hilary Clark). *Scenes of Shame; psychoanalysis, shame and writing*. Albany: State University of New York Press.

——— (1999) Guardian of the inmost me [In] Adamson and Clark (eds.). *Scenes of Shame*.

Anzieu, Didier (1959) *L'auto-analyse de Freud*. 2 vols. Paris: Presses Universitaires de France.

Aristotle [n.d. (1941)] *The Basic Works* (ed. Richard McKeon). New York: Random.

Armstrong, Francis (1990) Gender and miniaturization: games of littleness in nineteenth century fiction. *English Studies in Canada* 16(4).

Arnheim, Rudolph [1955 (1966)] A review of proportion [In] Gyorgy Kepes (ed.). *Module Proportion Symmetry, Rhythm*. New York: Braziller.

——— (1977) *The Dynamics of Architectural Form*. Berkeley: University of California Press.

Artemidoros [n.d. (1971)] *The Interpretation of Dreams (Oneirocritica)* (trans. and commentary Robert J. White). Park Ridge, N.J.: Noyes Press.

Balint, Michael (1968) *The Basic Fault*. London:Tavistock.

Baxter, John (1993) *Fellini*. New York: St. Martin's.

Benedict, Ruth (1946) *The Chrysanthemum and the Sword*. New York: Houghton.

165

Bentley, Eric [1946 (1986)] *The Pirandello Commentaries*. Evanston, Ill.: Northwestern University Press.

——— (1952) Introduction. *Naked Masks; five plays by Luigi Pirandello*. New York: Dutton.

Berenson, Bernard [1953 (1968)] *Seeing and Knowing*. London: Evelyn, Adams & Mackay.

Bergan, Ronald [1955 (1992)] *Jean Renoir: projections of paradise*. Woodstock, N.Y.: Overlook Press.

Bergler, Edmund [1953 (1987)] *Fashion and the Unconscious*. Madison, Conn.: International Universities Press.

Bergmann, Martin (1997) The tragic encounter between Freud and Ferenczi and its impact on the history of psychoanalysis [In] Rudnytsky et al (eds.). *Ferenczi's Turn in Psychoanalysis*.

Bion, W. R. (1959) Attacks on linking. *International Journal of Psychoanalysis* 40:308–318.

Bloomer, Kent C. and Moore, Charles W. (1977) *Body, Memory and Architecture*. New Haven: Yale University Press.

Blos, Peter (1974) The geneology of the ego ideal. *The Psychoanalytic Study of the Child* 29:43–88.

Blum, Howard (1994) The confusion of tongues and psychic trauma. *International Journal of Psychoanalysis* 75:871–882.

Bokanowski, Thierry (1996) Sandor Ferenczi: negative transference and transference depression [In] Rudnytsky et al. (eds.). *Ferenczi's Turn in Psychoanalysis*.

——— (1998) Entre Freud et Ferenczi: le traumatisme. *Revue Francaise de Psychoanalyse* 52:1285–1304.

Bonnet, Gerard (1996) *La violence de voir*. Paris: Presses Universitaires de France.

Bonomi, Carlo (1999) Flight into sanity. Jones's allegation of Ferenczi's mental deterioration reconsidered. *International Journal of Psychoanalysis* 80:507–542.

Brabant, E., Falzeder, E., and Giampieri-Deutsch, eds. (1992) *The Correspondence of Sigmund Freud and Sandor Ferenczi* (trans. Peter Hoffer). Cambridge: Harvard University Press.

Brazelton, T. B., Koslowski, N., and Main, M. (1974) The Origins of Reciprocity. The early mother-infant interaction [In] M. Lewis and L.

Rosenblum (eds.). *The Effect of the Infant on Its Caregiver.* New York: Wiley (pp. 49–76).

Britton, Ronald (1995) Psychic reality and unconscious belief. *International Journal of Psychoanalysis* 76:19–23.

Broucek, Frank (1991) *Shame and the Self.* New York: Guilford Press.

Busch, Thomas W. and Galligher, Shaun, eds. (1992) *Merleau-Ponty, hermeneutics and postmodernism.* Albany: State University of New York Press.

Caparrota, Luigi (1989) Some thoughts about the function of gaze avoidance in early infancy: a mother-baby observation. *Psychoanalytic Psychotherapy* 4:23–30.

Caputi, Anthony (1991) *Pirandello and the Crisis of Modern Consciousness.* Urbana: University of Illinois Press.

Carlyle, Thomas [1908 (1973)] *Sartor Resartus.* New York: Dutton Everyman's Library.

Carroll, Lewis [1862 (1991)] My Fancy. *The Complete Illustrated Lewis Carroll* (intro Alexander Woollcott). New York: Gallery Books.

——— [1865 (1991)] Alice in Wonderland. *The Complete Illustrated Lewis Carroll* (intro. Alexander Woollcott). New York: Gallery Books.

Chasseguet-Smirgel, Janine (1974) Perversion, idealization and sublimation. *International Journal of Psychoanalysis* 55:349–357.

——— (1976) Some thoughts on the ego-ideal; a contribution to the study of the "illness of ideality." *Psychoanalytic Quarterly.*

——— (1985) *The Ego Ideal.* New York: Norton.

Clair, Jean (1989) *Meduse: contribution à une anthropologie des arts du visuel.* Paris: Gallimard.

Clark, Hilary (1999) Depression, shame and reparation; the case of Anne Sexton [In] Adamson and Clark (eds.). *Scenes of Shame.*

Collins, James (1983) *The Mind of Kierkegaard.* Princeton N.J.: Princeton University Press.

Darwin, Charles (1872) *The Expression of Emotion in Men and Animals.* London: John Murray.

Demos, E. Virginia (1992) The early organization of the psyche [In] J. W. Bolton, M. N. Eagle, and D. L. Wolitsky (eds.). *Interface of Psychoanalysis and Psychology.* Washington, D.C.: American Psychological Association (pp. 200–232).

Derrida, Jacques (1967) *L'écriture de la difference.* Paris: Seuil.

—— (1990) *Memoires d'aveugle.* Paris: Eds de la Réunion des musees nationaux.

Devereux, George (1972) *Ethnopsychanalyse complémentariste.* Paris: Flamarion.

—— (1976a) *From Anxiety to Method in the Behavioral Sciences.* The Hague: Mouton.

—— (1976b) *Dreams in Greek Tragedy.* Oxford: Basil Blackwell.

—— (1980) *Basic Problems in Ethnopsychiatry.* Chicago: University of Chicago Press.

Dickens, Charles (1894) *The Writings of Charles Dickens.* 34 vols. New York: Houghton.

Dodds, E. R. (1951) *The Greeks and the Irrational.* Berkeley: University of California Press.

Doi, Takeo (1973) *The Anatomy of Dependence* (trans. John Bester). Tokyo: Kodansha International.

Dolis, John (1993) *The Style of Hawthorn's Gaze: regarding subjectivity.* Tuscaloosa: University of Alabama Press.

Dupont, Judith (1994) Freud's analysis of Ferenczi as revealed by their correspondence. *International Journal of Psychoanalysis* 75:301–320.

Durkheim, Emile [1912 (1968)] *Les formes élementaires de la vie religieuse.* Paris: Presses Universitaires de France.

Edelstein, E. and L. (1945) *Asclepius.* 2 vols. Baltimore: Johns Hopkins.

Ellison, Ralph (1990) *The Invisible Man.* New York: Random (Vintage).

Erikson, Eric H. (1950) *Childhood and Society.* New York: W. W. Norton.

Federn, Paul (1952) *Ego Psychology and the Psychoses.* New York: Basic Books.

Fenichel, Otto (1945) *The Psychoanalytic Theory of Neurosis.* New York: Norton.

Ferenczi, Sandor (1913) On eye symbolism [In] *The Selected Papers of Sandor Ferenczi* (1950). vol. 1, pp. 270–276. New York: Basic.

—— (1926) Embarassed hands [In] *The Selected Papers of Sandor Ferenczi.* vol. 2, pp. 315–316. London: Hogarth Press.

—— (1927) Gulliver phantasies [In] *The Selected Papers of Sandor Ferenczi* (1955). vol. 3, pp. 41–60. New York: Basic.

—— [1933 (1955)] The confusion of tongues; the language of tenderness and of passion [In] Michael Balint (ed.). *The Selected Papers of Sandor Ferenczi.* vol 3. New York: Basic.

—— (1950) *The Selected Papers of Sandor Ferenczi.* vol. 1 (intro. Clara Thompson). New York: Basic.

—— [1985 (1988)] *The Clinical Diary of Sandor Ferenczi* (ed. Judith Dupont, and trans. Michael Balint and Nicola Zarday Jackson). Cambridge: Harvard University Press.

Fox, Richard P. (1998) Unobjectionable countertransference. *Journal of the American Psychoanalytic Association* 46(4):1067–1088.

Freud, Sigmund [*Standard Edition* (1974). 25 vols. London: Hogarth Press.]

—— (1899) On Screen Memories. *SE* 3:301–322.

—— (1900–1901) The Interpretation of Dreams. *SE* 4–5.

—— (1905) Three Essays on a Theory of Sexuality. *SE* 7:130–243.

—— (1910) Psychogenic Disturbance of Vision. *SE* 11: 209–218.

—— (1914a) On Narcissism, an introduction. *SE* 14:73–102.

—— (1914b) Remembering, Repeating and Working-Through. *SE*12: 145–156.

—— (1915a) Instincts and Their Vicissitudes. *SE* 14: 110–140.

—— (1915b) The Unconscious. *SE* 14: 160–215.

—— [1917 (1915)] Mourning and Melancholia. *SE* 14:239–258.

—— (1920) Beyond the Pleasure Principle. *SE* 18: 201–64.

—— (1921) Group Psychology and the Analysis of the Ego. *SE* 18: 69–143.

—— (1923) The Ego and the Id. *SE* 19:12–66.

—— (1924) The Economic Problem of Masochism. *SE* 19:157–172.

—— (1926) Inhibitions, Symptoms, and Anxiety. *SE* 20:87–175.

—— (1930) Civilization and Its Discontents. *SE* 21:64–145.

Gabbard, Glen (1977) The vissitudes of shame in stage fright [In] C. W. Socarides and S. Kramer (eds.). *Work and Its Inhibitions; psychoanalytic essays.* Madison, Ct.: International Universities Press.

—— (1979) Stage Fright. *International Journal of Psychoanalysis* 60:383–392.

—— (1983) Further contributions to the understanding of stage fright: narcissistic issues. *Journal of the American Psychoanalytic Association* 31: 423–444.

Goffman, E. (1959) *The Presentation of Self in Everyday Life*. Garden City, N.Y.: Anchor.

Gogol, Nikolai [1842a (1999)] The Nose, *the Collected Tales of Nicolai Gogol* (trans. Richard Peavear and Larissa Volokhonsky). New York: Random (Vintage).

—— [1842b (1999)] The Overcoat, *The Collected Tales of Nicolai Gogol* (trans. Richard Peavear and Larissa Volokhonsky). New York: Random (Vintage).

—— [1842c (1997)] *Dead Souls* (trans. Richard Peavear and Larissa Volokhonsky). New York: Random (Vintage).

Goldberg, Carl (1991) *Understanding Shame*. New York: Jason Aronson.

Goldberger, Marianne (1995) The couch as defense and as potential for enactment. *Psychoanalytic Quarterly* 64(1)23–42.

Greenacre, Phyllis (1955) *Swift and Carroll: a psychoanalytyic study of two lives*. New York: International Universities Press.

Grunberger, Bela (1979) *Narcissism*. New York: International Universities Press.

Hargreaves-Mawdsley, W. N. (1963) *A History of Legal Dress in Europe until the End of the Eighteenth Century*. Oxford: Oxford University Press.

Hawthorne, Nathanial [1850 (1993)] *The Scarlet Letter*. Oxford: Oxford University Press.

Haynal, André (1997) Freud and his intellectual environment; the case of Sandor Ferenczi [In] Rudnytsky et al (eds.). *Ferenczi's Turn in Psychoanalysis*.

Hegel, G. W. F. [1807 (1977)] *Phenomenology of the Spirit* (trans. A. V. Miller). Oxford: Oxford University Press.

Hoffer, Axel (1985) Towards a definition of analytic neutrality. *Journal of the American Psychoanalytical Association* 33:771–795.

—— (1997) Asymmetry and mutuality in the analytic relgionship: contemporary lessons from the Freud-Ferenczi dialogue [In] Rudnytsky et al (eds.). *Ferenczi's Turn in Psychoanalysis*.

Hollander, Ann [1975 (1977)] *Seeing Through Clothes*. New York: Viking.

Josephs, Lawrence (1997) The view from the tip of the Iceberg. *Journal of the American Psychoanalytic Association* 45(2): 425–464.

Kafka, Franz [1925 (1984)] *The Trial*. New York: Knopf.

—— (1971) The Hunger Artist [In] Natham Glazer (ed.). *Franz Kafka The Complete Stories*. New York: Schoken.

Kant, Immanuel [1790 (1978)] *The Critique of Judgement* (trans. James Meredith). Oxford: Oxford University Press.

—— [1781 (1896)] *Critique of Pure Reason* (trans. Max Muller). London: Macmillan.

—— (1977) *Prolegomena to Any Future Metaphysics* (trans, Paul Carus). Indianapolis: Hackett Publishing Co.

Kepes, Gyorgy, ed. (1966) *Module, Proportion, Symmetry, Rhythm*. 4 vols. New York: Braziller.

Kernberg, Otto (1975) *Borderline Conditions and Pathological Narcisism*. New York: Jason Aronson.

Kierkegaard, Soren *Either/Or* [1843(1959)] (trans. Walter Lowrie). 2 vols. Garden City, N.Y.: Doubleday.

—— [1849 (1989)] *The Sickness Unto Death* (trans. Alistair Hannay). London: Penguin.

—— *The Concept of Dread* [1855(1944)] (trans. Walter Lowrie). Princeton, N.J.: Princeton University Press.

—— *The Concept of Anxiety* (1980) (ed. and trans. R. Thomte). Princeton, N.J.: Princeton University Press.

Kilborne, Benjamin (1978) *Intérpretation du rêve au Maroc*. Claix: La Pensée Sauvage.

—— (1981a) Pattern, structure and style in anthropological studies of dreams. *Ethos* 9(2):165–185.

—— (1981b) Aspects of the handling of symbols in Moroccan dream interpretation. *Psychoanalytic Study of Society* 9:1–14.

—— (1981c) Dream interpretation and culturally constituted defense mechanisms. *Ethos* 9(4): 294–312.

—— (1982) Anthropological thought in France in the wake of the revolution: La Societé des Observateurs de l'Homme. *European Archives of Sociology* 23: 73–91.

———— (1987a) In memoriam: George Devereux. *Psychoanalytic Study of Society* 11:1–14.

———— (1987b) On classifying dreams [In] Barbara Tedlock (ed.). *Dreaming: anthropological and psychological interpretations.* Cambridge: Cambridge University Press.

———— (1992a) Fields of shame; anthropologists abroad. *Ethos* 20(2): 230–253.

———— (1992b) Positivism and its vicissitudes: the role of faith in the social sciences. *Journal of the History of the Behavioral Sciences* 28(3): 352–370.

———— (1995a) Truths which cannot go naked; a review essay. *Psychiatry* 58:278–297.

———— (1995b) Of creatures large and small: psychic size, size anxiety, and the analytic situation. *Psychoanalytic Quarterly* 64: 672–690.

———— (1997) The hunting of the red-faced snark [In] Melvin Lansky and Andrew Morrison (eds.). *The Widening Scope of Shame.* Hillsdale, N.J.: Analytic Press.

———— (1998a) Ferenczi, regression and shame. *International Forum of Psychoanalysis* 7:225–228.

———— (1998b) The disappearing who [In] Joseph Adamson and Hilary Clark (eds.). *Scenes of Shame: psychoanalysis, shame and writing.* Albany: State University of New York Press.

———— (1999a) When trauma strikes the soul. *American Journal of Psychoanalysis* 59(4):385–403.

———— (1999b) Wrestling with Proteus. *Psychoanalytic Inquiry* 19(3): 362–372.

———— (2001) Shame deeper, deepest: shame [In] *The Scarlet Letter* (unpublished paper).

Kilborne, Benjamin and Degarrod, Lydia N. (1983) As in a Dream: some paintings of Giorgio de Chirico. *Dreamworks* 3(4):281–293.

King, David (1997) *The Commisar Vanishes; the falsification of photographs and art in Stalin's Russia.* New York: Henry Holt.

Kirmmsew, Bruce H. (1990) *Kierkegaard in Golden Age Denmark.* Bloomington: Indiana University Press.

Kirschner, Lewis (1993) Concepts of reality and psychic reality in psychoanalysis as illustrated by the disagreement between Freud and Ferenczi. *International Journal of Psychoanalysis* 75: 219–230.

Kohut, Heinz (1971) *The Analysis of the Self.* New York: International Universities Press.

—— (1977) *The Restoration of the Self.* New York: International Universities Press.

—— (1984) *How Does Analysis Cure?* Arnold Goldberg (ed.). Chicago: University of Chicago Press.

Krausz, Rosmarie (1994) The invisible woman. *International Journal of Psychoanalysis* 79:59–72.

Kris, Anton O. (1982) *Free Association: method and process.* New Haven/London: Yale University Press.

Kundera, Milan (1995) *The New York Review of Books* (Sept. 21).

Lacan, Jacques (1966) *Écrits* (trans. A. Sheridan). New York: Norton.

Lanes, Selma G. (1980) *The Art of Maurice Sendak.* New York: Abagale Press (Henry Abrams).

Lansky, Melvin (1992) *Fathers Who Fail.* Hillsdale, N.J.: Analytic Press.

—— (1996) Shame and suicide in Sophocles' Ajax. *Psychoanalytic Quarterly* 65:761–786.

—— (1997) (with Andrew Morrison, ed.). *The Widening Scope of Shame.* Hillsdale, N.J.: Analytic Press.

Lansky, Melvin and Morrison, Andrew (1997) The legacy of Freud's writings on shame [In] Melvin Lansky and Andrew Morrison (eds.). *The Widening Scope of Shame.*

Laplanche, Jean, and Pontalis, J. B. (1981) *Vocabulaire de la Psychanalyse.* Paris: Presses Universitaires de France.

Lasch, Christopher (1978) *The Culture of Narcissism.* New York: Norton.

Laver, James [1969 (1982)] *Costume and Fashion: a concise history.* London: Thames and Hudson.

LeCoque, Andre (1987) *Encyclopedia of Religion* (ed. Mircea Eliade). New York: Macmillan.

Leonardo Da Vinci (1938) *The Notebooks of Leonardo DaVinci* (ed. Edward MacCurdy). London: Macmillan.

—— (1945) *The Drawings of Leonardo da Vinci* (ed. A. E. Popham). New York: Harcourt.

Lewis, C. S. *The Chronicles of Narnia.*

Lewis, Helen Block (1971) *Shame and Guilt in Neurosis*. New York: International Universities Press.

Lewis, Michael (1992) *Shame: the exposed self*. Glencoe, Scotland: Free Press.

Levy, Steven T. and Inderbitzin, Larence B. (1997) Safety, danger and analytic authority. *Journal of the American Psychoanalytic Association* 45(2):377–394.

Lynd, Helen (1958) *On Shame and the Search for Identity*. New York: Harcourt.

Mahoney, Patrick (1989) Aspects of nonperverse scopophilia within an analysis. *Journal of the American Psychoanalytic Association* 37(2): 365–400.

Martin-Cabré, Luis J. (1997) Freud-Ferenczi: controversy terminable and interminable. *International Journal of Psychoanalysis* 30:69–74.

Marvell, Andrew [1681 (1972)] *Complete Poems*. Penguin.

Matthaei, Renate (1973) *Luigi Pirandello* (trans. Somon and Erika Young). New York: Ungar.

Mauss, Marcel (1967) *The Gift: forms and functions of exchange in archaic societies* (trans. Ian Cunnison). New York: Norton.

Mellinkoff, Ruth (1993) *Outcasts: signs of otherness in Northern European art of the Late Middle Ages*. 2 vols. Berkeley: University of California Press.

Melville, Herman (1988) *Moby Dick, or the Whale*. Evanston Ill.: Northwestern University Press.

Merleau-Ponty, Maurice (1964) *Le visible et l'invisible*. Paris: Tel.

Miller, William (1993) *Humiliation*. Ithaca: Cornell University Press.

Milton, John (1640–1665) *Paradise Lost*.

—— (1640–1670) *Samson Agonistes*.

—— (1941) *The Complete Poetical Works* (ed. Harris Francis Fletcher). Cambridge, Mass.: Riverside Press.

Morrison, Andrew (1989) *Shame the Underside of Narcissism*. Hillsdale, N.J.: Analytic Press.

—— (1996) *The Culture of Shame*. Hillsdale, N.Y.: Ballantine Books.

Nagel, Julie J. (1998) Injury and pain in performing musicians: a psychodynamic diagnosis. *Bulletin of the Menninger Clinic* 62(1):83–95.

———— (1999) The Paradox of Performance Anxiety in Musicians: the delusion of omnipotence (unpublished paper).

Nagel, Thomas (1998) The shredding of public privacy; reflections on recent events in Washington. *Times Literary Supplement*, August 14, 1998.

Nathanson, Donald, ed. (1987) *The Many Faces of Shame*. New York: Guilford Press.

Novick, K. K. and Novick, J. (1991) Some comments on masochism and the delusion of omnipotence from a developmental perspective. *Journal of the American Psychoanalytic Association* 39:307–331.

———— (1992) *Shame and Pride: affect, sex and the birth of the self*. New York: Norton.

Pagels, Elaine (1988) *Adam, Eve and the Serpent*. New York: Random.

Peristiany, J. B. (1965) *Honour and Shame: the values of Mediterranean society*. London: Weidenfeld and Nicolson.

Piers, G and Singer, M [1953 (1971)] *Shame and Guilt*. New York: Norton.

Pirandello, Luigi (1926) *The Notebooks of Serafino Gubbio, Cinematograph Operator, or Shoot* (trans. C. K. Scott-Moncrieff.). New York: Dutton.

———— (1928) *The Old and the Young*, 2 vols. (trans. C. K. Scott-Moncrieff). New York: Dutton.

———— (1931) *As You Desire Me (Come tu mi vuoi). a play in three acts* (trans. Samuel Putnam). New York: Dutton.

———— (1933) *One, None and a Hundred Thousand* (trans. Samuel Putnam). New York: Dutton.

———— (1952) *Naked Masks; five plays by Luigi Pirandello* (ed. Eric Bentley). New York: Dutton.

———— (1964) *The Late Mattia Pascal* (trans. William Weaver). London: Andre Deutsch.

———— (1988) *Pirandello Collected Plays*, vol. 2. New York: Riverrun Press.

———— (1994) *Eleven Short Stories* (undici novelle) (trans. Stanley Appelbaum). New York: Dover Publications.

———— *A passing touch* (story).

Plato, *The Collected Dialogues* (1961) (eds. Edith Hamilton and Huntinton Cairns). Princeton (Bollingen): Princeton University Press.

Poland, Warren S. (1992) Transference: an original creation. *Psychoanalytic Quarterly* 59 (2) 185–205.

Quindlin, Anna (1994) The price of privacy. *The New York Times*, September 28, 1994.

Rapaport, David (1957) A theoretical analysis of the superergo concept [In] *Collected Papers of David Rapaport* (ed. Merton Gill). New York: Basic.

Rangell, Leo (1954) "The psychology of poise, with a special elaboration on the psychic significance of the snout or periorial region." *International Journal of Psychoanalysis* 35:313–333.

—— (1963) The scope of intrapsychic conflict: microscopic and macroscopic considerations. *Psychoanalytic Study of the Child*. New Haven: Yale University Press (vol. 18, pp. 75–102).

Renik, Owen (1995) The ideal of the anonymous analyst and the problem of self-disclosure. *Psychoanalytic Quarterly* 64(2):466–495.

—— (1996) The perils of neutrality. *Psychoanalytic Quarterly* 65(3): 495–517.

—— (1998) The analyst's subjectivity and the analyst's objectivity. *International Journal of Psychoanalysis* 79:487–497.

Ricoeur, Paul (1967) *The Symbolism of Evil*. Boston: Little Brown.

Rilke, Rainer Maria (1985) *Letters on Cezanne* (ed. Clara Rilke and trans. Joel Agee). New York: Fromm International Publishing Co.

—— [1949 (1992)] *Notebooks of Malte Laurids Brigge* (trans. M. D. Herter Norton). New York: Norton.

Rizzuto, Ana-Maria (1991) Shame in psychoanalysis: the function of unconscious fantasies. *International Journal of Psychoanalysis* 72:297–312.

Rosenbaum, Ron (1994) The spy who created the cold [In] *New York Times Magazine*, July 10, 1994, pp. 29ff.

Roudinesco, Elizabeth (1986) *Jacques Lacan & Co.; a history of psychoanalysis in France, 1925–1985*. Chicago: University of Chicago Press.

Rudnysky, Peter, Bokoy, Antal, and Giampieri-Deutsch, eds. (1996) *Ferenczi's Turn in Psychoanalysis*. New York: New York University Press.

Rushdie, Salman (1983) *Shame*. New York: Knopf.

—— (1996) *New York Times Book Review*, October 6, 1996.

Sartre, Jean-Paul (1964) *Being and Nothingness* (trans. Hazel E. Barnes). New York: Citadel Press.

——— (1975) *The Emotions; outline of a theory.* Secaucus, N.J.

——— (1983) *Cahiers pour une morale.* Paris: Gallimard.

Schilder, Paul (1950) *The Image and Appearance of the Human Body.* New York: International Universities Press.

——— (1972) Psychoanalytic remarks on Alice in Wonderland and Lewis Carroll [In] R. Phillips (ed.). *Aspects of Alice.* London: Gollanz.

Sheldon, Michael (1994) *Graham Greene; the man within.* London: Heineman.

Scheff, Thomas and Retzinger, Susan (1991) *Emotions and Violence.* Lexington, Mass.: Lexington Books.

Schneider, Carl (1977) *Shame, Exposure and Privacy.* Boston: Beacon.

Sendak, Maurice. *Where The Wild Things Are.*

Siebert, Charles (1996) The cuts that go deeper. *New York Times Magazine,* July 7, 1997.

Silber, A. (1976) Review of C. Allen, The fear of looking or scopophilic-exhibitionistic conflicts. Psychoanalytic *Quarterly* 45:634–637.

Simon, Bennett (1988) *Tragic Drama and the Family; psychoanalytic studies from Aeschylus to Beckett.* New Haven: Yale University Press.

Snell, Bruno (1953) *The Discovery of the Mind.* Cambridge: Harvard University Press.

Sophocles (1957) "Oedipus Rex" (trans. John Morre). *Sophocles II* (eds. David Greene and Richmond Lattimore). Chicago: University of Chicago Press.

——— (1957) "Philoctetes" (trans. David Green) *Sophocles II* (eds. David Greene and Richmond Lattimore). Chicago: University of Chicago Press.

——— (1957) "Ajax" (trans. John Moore) *Sophocles II* (eds. David Greene and Richmond Lattimore). Chicago: University of Chicago Press.

Spiro, Melford (1987) Religious systems as culturally constituted defense mechanisms [In] Benjamin Kilborne and L. L. Langness (eds.). *Culture and Human Nature: theoretical papers of Melford E. Spiro.* Chicago: University of Chicago Press.

Spitz, Rene (1950) Anxiety in infancy. a study of its manifestations in the first year of life. *International Journal of Psychoanalysis*, 31.

—— (1957) *No and Yes: on the genesis of human communication*. New York: International Universities Press.

—— (1965) *The First Year of Life*. New York: International Universities Press.

Starobinski, Jean (1961) *L'oeil vivant*. Paris: Gallimard.

Stewart, Kilton (1954) *Pygmies and Dream Giants*. London: Victor Gollanez.

Swift, Jonathan [1726 (1967)] *Gulliver's Travels*. London: Penguin.

Tisseron, Serge (1992) *La Honte: psychanalyse d'un lien social*. Paris: Dunod.

Tolstaya, Tatyana (1998) Missing persons. *New York Review of Books*, January 15, 1998.

Tomkins, Sylvan (1962) *Affect, Imagery, Consciousness*. vol. 1: The Positive Affects. New York: Springer.

—— (1963) *Affect, Imagery, Consciousness*. vol 2: The Negative Affects. New York: Springer.

—— (1991) *Affect, Imagery, Consciousness*. vol 3: The Negative Affects (Anger and Fear). New York: Springer.

Tronick, Adamson, L, Wise, S., and Brazelton, T. (1978) The infant's response to entrapment between contradictory messages in face-to-face interaction. *Journal of Child Psychiatry* 17:1–13.

Updike, John (1971) Foreward to *Franz Kafka The Complete Stories*. New York: Schoken.

Van der Velde, C. D. (1985) Body images of one's self and of others: developmental and clinical significance. *American Journal of Psychiatry* 142:527–537.

Vernant, Jean-Pierre (1985) *La mort dans les yeux*. Paris: Hachette.

Vincent, John Martin (1935) *Costume and Conduct in the Laws of Basel, Bern and Zurich 1370–1800*. Baltimore: Johns Hopkins.

Weissman, S. (1977) Face to face: the role of vision and smiling response. *Psychoanalysis Study Child* 32:421–450.

Westermarck, Edward (1901) *The History of Human Marriage*. London: Macmillan.

——— (1926) *Ritual and Belief in Morocco.* 2 vols. London and New York: Macmillan.

Williams, Bernard (1993) *Shame and Necessity.* Berkeley: University of California Press.

Winnicott, D. W. (1953) Transitional objects and transitional phenomena. *International Journal of Psychoanalysis* 34:89–97.

——— (1958) The capacity to be alone [In] *The Maturational Processes and the Facilitating Environment.* London: Hogarth Press.

Wollheim, Richard (1999) *On the Emotions.* New Haven: Yale University Press.

Wurmser, Leon (1981) *The Mask of Shame.* Baltimore: Johns Hopkins.

——— (1987) Shame: the veiled companion of narcissism [In] Nathanson, *Many Faces* (pp. 64–92).

——— (1997) The shame about existing: a comment about the analysis of "moral" masochism [In] Lansky and Morrison (eds.). *Widening Scope of Shame* (pp. 367–382).

Zimmer, Henri (1997) Corregio. *New York Review of Books,* September 25, 1997.

Index

Abandonment, 2, 27; anxiety, 8484; childhood, 27, 54; fear of, 65, 66, 84, 93; by God, 84; maternal, 66; of Oedipus, 2, 7–8; parental, 52, 54; shame of, 120

Adam and Eve, 83, 84, 158*n*13; abandoned by God, 84, 89; dissimulation by, 87; envied by Satan, 85–86; Oedipal defeat of, 84

Adamson, Joseph, 100

Aegisthus, 37

Aggression: guilt and, 2

Aidos, 38–39

Ajax, 2, 38

Alice in Wonderland (Carroll), 9–10, 14, 21, 23, 62, 121

Alienation, 32, 123

Allegory of the cave, 46

Amplificato, 16–17

Anagnorisis, 83

Anderson, Hans Christian, 104

Anger, 39; at abandonment, 67; in infancy, 4

Annihilation, 55

Anomie, 150*n*2

Anonymity: fantasies of, 27

Anxiety: abandonment, 8484; in analysis, 28; annihilation, 65; at

being misperceived, 56; of being unrecognizable, 47–48; blindness and, 43; castration, 110; clothing and, 110; control and, 40; imagining oneself through other's eyes and, 10; of loss, 92; over exclusion, 84; performance, 45–60; separation, 84; size, 18–21, 136*n*1; toleration of, 35; transformation of, 35

Anxiety, appearance, xii, 3–5; avoidance of conflict and, 29; as cultural phenomenon, 5; media and, 5; observation and, 5–6; perception and, 7; plastic surgery and, 5; repression and, 123; sources of, 13

Aphrodite, 38

Appearance: anxiety, xii, 3–5, 13, 29, 123; connivance and, 124–125; contemporary emphasis on, 8; control of, 5, 10, 34, 43, 123, 130; cultural illusion and, 5; dependence on, 123; dynamics of, 40, 58, 109–110; fantasies, 110; of hiding something, 42; hiding unacceptable, 6; humiliation and, 110; illusions of, 75; imagined, 109; instability of, 89; keeping up,

181